DEAR CHRISTOPHER

Letters to Christopher Columbus by
Contemporary Native Americans

Edited by
Darryl Wilson and Barry Joyce

Native American Studies
University of California, Riverside

1992

To Hoss and Boss
For Angela and Joseph

This publication was made possible in part through funds provided by Pacific Bell.

Copyright © 1992
Regents of the University of California

ISBN 0-9635573-0-0

Manufactured in the United States of America.

PREFACE

The past five hundred years has not been kind to the native people of this land. It is tantamount to a holocaust brought on by the military, religious and biological invasion of the land by European nations and the continuance of this tragedy by Euro-Americans. The historical record on this is clear. The conquest of this land was followed by a resettlement of its native people by a new population which prospered on native land, sometimes with the use of native labor. The invasion and conquest reached deep into the Native American communities of this land, affecting nearly every aspect of traditional life. The first people of this land still feel the impact of the destruction, and they share a "blood memory" of the way in which the conquest influenced their tribes, clans, and families. But in spite of it all, native peoples survived, and a small number of them have shared their thoughts through this publication.

Dear Christopher is not an attempt to chronicle the many wrongs perpetrated against American Indians during the past five hundred years, for such a task is impossible. It is a voice for contemporary American Indians, one of many that has been heard in 1992. The book is a voice of several Native Americans who chose to open their hearts through their stories, comments, poems, and memoirs. We have endeavored to keep the letters essentially as they came to use, changing only minor grammatical errors and formatting the letters so that they are uniform in presentation. We both owe a debt of gratitude to several people for making this book possible. Together we thank Chancellor Raymond Orbach and Dean Brian Copenhaver for their continued support of Native American Studies at the University of California, Riverside. We thank Clifford E. Trafzer, Chair of Ethnic Studies and Director of Native American Studies who is serving as Series Editor of Publications in Native

American Studies at the University of California, Riverside.

In addition, we thank Pamela Norman, Eufemia Reyes Moore, and Lee Ann Smith-Trafzer for setting the type and formatting this volume. Darryl Wilson wishes to thank Hoss and Boss for giving him the time to work, and Jay Stauss and the students and staff of American Indian Studies at the University of Arizona for their continued support of his educational efforts. Barry Joyce thanks James Nauman for his teamwork and editing assistance as well as his colleagues at Cabrillo National Monument for offering various aspects of the Quincentennial. Wilson thanks the native peoples of California who have encouraged him to research and write, while Joyce extends his appreciation to the Kumeyaay people of San Diego County for sharing their heritage with him, particularly Ron Christman and Jane Dumas. We both have enjoyed working with the authors of the letters, and we thank them one and all for sharing their words with us.

Darryl Wilson
Tucson, Arizona

Barry Joyce
San Diego, California

INTRODUCTION

Before "time," when the earth was very young, the world was filled only with water. It was a magical time but one of great emptiness. On the endless ocean of blue water, Earthmaker and Coyote floated on a raft. They floated forever, moving with the rhythm of the water, the waves pushing them to and fro in many different directions. Coyote seemed content with this, but Earthmaker thought of something. In a vision he first saw the earth, solid land with mountains, rivers, plants, and animals. In his dream he saw hills and valleys with fog drifting in and out of the area with the changes of each day. In his wisdom, Earthmaker saw a world with solid land where the earth, plants, animals, wind, and wonder worked together. This was the creation he saw, so he put the promise into motion with his song.

Earthmaker sat at the front of the raft and sang his song of creation. Over and over again he sang his song.

> Little world, where are you? Little world, where are you? My world of great mountains, where are you? My foggy mountains, where are you?

> My world, where one will travel by the valley's edge, by great foggy mountains, by the zigzag paths through range after range. I sing of the country I shall travel in. In this world I shall wander.

Earthmaker sang until he became tired. He had the vision of creation and the song, but still the season was not right. He asked Coyote to sing the song of creation, and Coyote did, standing at the front of the raft singing out his heart for some time. When Coyote became tired, he told Earthmaker, "This is your song, you sing it."

So Earthmaker sang out again, sang of the Little World he had seen in his vision. Not long after, Earthmaker saw Robin with a small round nest floating in the blue water. "Upon this small basket," Earthmaker said of Robin's nest,, "I shall make the world, put it into motion, as I have seen in my vision." Robin joined in the singing--the sweet song we still hear Robin sing today. While Robin sang, Earthmaker took large ropes, attached one end to the nest and pulled the others out into the four directions.

As Robin sang, Earthmaker reached down into the depths of the water, taking handfuls of mud, fashioning it into the hills, mountains, and valleys. He caused the plants to grow and molded animal people from clay and water. He began the process of creation. This was not an event completed in six days but a process that Earthmaker put into motion. The plants, animals, waters, and landforms interacted with each other, bringing life into this new world. Earthmaker and Robin prepared the earth for the native people who would one day live in this land.

The plants and animals, the rivers and mountains lived first, but they knew of humans and they made ready for the people that Earthmaker would create in prayer and song. When natives emerged into this land, they did not place themselves above the plants and animals, the rivers or mountains. They did not assume to have dominion over the trees, roots, fish, fowl, or game. They were grateful to be a part of the creation, and they lived as brothers and sisters with the spirits that dwelled within the animate and inanimate beings of this land. Coyote had seen the creation, and he was part of it as well. Yet all was not to be positive, since there were counterbalancing charges in the creation. There was positive and negative, male and female, wet and dry spells, and many other dualities.

As time unfolded the plants and animal people played out their dramas with the first people of the land. These native people had a great deal of respect for the plant and animal people, learned their history and told and retold that history in their oral tradition as it became a part of their own cultures, beliefs, philosophies, and spiritual precepts. The interaction of these people unfolded for hundreds of years before other new peoples arrived. By far the most important of these first newcomers was from Genoa, Italy. His name was Christopher Columbus, and his four voyages would change the history of the earth forever.

Much has been written about Columbus the man, the mariner, and the explorer, nearly all in a positive light. While scholars have long known of the invasion, conquest, enslavement, and brutality of Spanish exploration, Columbus has somehow escaped the stain of the *black legend* that sprang from the documentation of Bartolomé de Las Casas in the 16th century. In fact, Columbus, probably owing to his obscure origins, was adopted early as the symbol of western "civilization." Nowhere was this view more warmly embraced than in the United States. Columbus's first major biographer, Washington Irving, in the 19th century, extolled the virtues of Columbus as the symbol of an emerging new nation. Later that same century, the eminent historian, George Bancroft, credited Columbus with being the catalyst for the fulfillment of God's divine and manifest plan for America, a latter-day patriarch à la Abraham or Moses. In 1892, Columbus became a figurehead for that paean to the progress of American civilization known as the Chicago Columbian Exposition. He was again resurrected in 1942 by Samuel Eliot Morison as a balm for a nation suffering through the dark days of World War II, giving his readers a chance to lose themselves within Morison's "manly" depiction of the quintessential swashbuckling, adventurous Admiral of the Ocean Seas. In these accounts, America was depicted as a "wild" land filled with "savage" people who had no true language, culture, government, or religion.

Thus the conquest has been viewed in most texts as something positive. Generations of Americans have been provided with this false information and have been raised with no knowledge of the American holocaust that began with the arrival of Columbus. The textbooks are silent on Columbus' role in the ruthless slaughter of thousands of Native Americans.   The public is unaware of the kidnapping of women and children, taken as hostages in exchange for gold and often murdered by their captors. Little or no information has circulated to lay readers about the large-scale brutalization of of Native Americans who were the first slaves of this land, people who became strangers in their own homelands.

During the years of Columbus-as-protagonist, few stopped to listen for contrary voices of opinion. But finally, other voices *were* heard, the ancestral voices of those living along the shores of San Salvador Island, Vera Cruz, Pit River, Plymouth Rock, and many other sites, testifying to the tragedy inflicted upon their people by Columbus and those who followed. As a result, new voices are now calling out for the "heroic" Columbus to be brought down from the silver screen of celluloid fantasy, out of equally fanciful history books, and purged from elementary readers in order to expose the Columbus myth to the piercing light of judgement.

As the world prepares to "celebrate" or "commemorate" the quincentenary of the first voyage of Columbus, we have asked Native Americans to respond to Columbus in their own way. We have asked American Indians this question: "If you had an opportunity to write Christopher Columbus, what would you say to him?" Some have written a letter in narrative form. Some have offered their own interpretations of the "discovery" and conquest.   Some have written poetry to help others understand their feelings. Some have written prose and stories to convey their thoughts. In some small way *Dear Christopher* will provide American Indians with a new voice, one that will be heard over the celebration of some and the mourning of others.

Dear Christopher:

I suppose you know your big holiday is arriving to mixed reviews here in America. Don't worry, I'm not writing to heap abuse on you, just to let you know about some of the results of your voyage of 500 years ago. Lots of things have changed, of course, but attitudes towards the indigenous peoples of America still bear a great deal of resemblance to those you first expressed in your now famous diary. Although you probably wouldn't recognize me with clothes on, I'm one of the descendants of those "Indians" who went around "quite naked as their mothers bore them;" you know, one of those you judged would "be good servants" who, you claimed, would easily be made Christians because they "belonged to no religion."

Views on native religions, Christopher, have taken some notable twists and turns since your most regrettable faux pas, but all the "takes" on native religions have really amounted to seeing native spirituality as a curiosity rather than a valid set of belief systems. Native religions have been regarded (as you regarded them) as non existent and, in turn, as primitive and dangerous, and as readily imitated. Most recently they seem to be regarded as a wonderful commodity. The other day as I stood in line in a local bookstore, two teen-age girls came in to look at some prepackaged life-changing visionary cards. As I looked on, they pulled out two sets that were for sale (one professing to be based on Native American religion and philosophy). After a glance at each tarot-like deck, they rejected the "Native American" set as having the least attractive pictures and purchased the other. That's all I saw, Christopher. Just then I couldn't bring myself to look more closely at what was being sold in that store. Whatever it was, I knew it had been stolen, altered and commercialized beyond recognition; and I knew that it would always be more accepted than the truth.

For one thing that might surprise you, Christopher, is that after all this time most people still know very little about indigenous peoples. I know this because I work as a college teacher (I guess you *were* right about one thing, Colon,--Native Americans can "repeat very quickly whatever is said to them," which, unfortunately, is one of the major requirements of becoming a college professor.) Anyway, as I was telling you, people know so little beyond popular stereotypes about native peoples. In two of my first job interviews at "universities of higher learning" I was offered the answer to what it was assumed would be a burning concern of any Indian--where will I board my horse? I took this kindly, Christopher, as I have learned to take most of the absurd encounters that Indian people are heir to. But it confirmed for me that the death of Native American stereotypes has been greatly exaggerated. The most popular stereotype, of course, is that there are no more Indians. Of course, this idea that tribal people have vanished often has them disappearing as if by magic, disappearing inevitably or as in the proper course of things; never does it depict the treachery of scorched earth campaigns (interesting parallel to Saddam Hussein's methods of destruction, don't you think?), the distribution of small-pox-infested blankets, and the out and out military massacres of unarmed women and children (My Lai-style?). And if the Indian Wars must be admitted and spoken of they are justified by another popular stereotype--the demon savage. Who could be on the side of the tribal people in the Cowboy and Indian versions of the story: peaceful god-fearing settlers traveling westward with a wagon train full of good people attacked without cause by ugly heathens who scalp their victims, who steal and enslave women and children?

Because, Christopher, among the things that haven't changed since your arrival is the dissemination of false information about native peoples. Yes, it has really become quite an industry here in America. Lots of people since you have made their living writing just whatever they please about Native Americans, or whatever would most please their audiences. Perhaps you will be happy to know though that through the years, all the changing rhetoric amounts to nothing more than an echo of the declarations of possession you made 500 years ago. The precedents you set--your view of the people in financial rather than human terms, your view of the land as thing rather than being, your view of both as commodity--these precedents have yet to be overturned.

A lot of people, for example, made pretty good military and political careers following your lead in Indian affairs, believing as you did that tribal peoples "could all be subjected and made to do all that one wished." What was wished most vehemently in the early years was that indigenous people vacate the premises. So the treatment of the human commodity changed a little for a time, and many leaders claimed not that American Indians would be good servants (as you did), but that they were good for nothing and should be exterminated (just as any of the other commodities of the new world like the buffalo and the native timber were decimated when they got in the way of the "progress of civilization"). One of the most famous statements of this era came from General Philip Sheridan: "The only good Indians I ever saw were dead." Sheridan's statement in a slightly altered version has become one of the stock phrases of any self-respecting Indian-hater and has probably been recited more often than the golden rule: "The only good Indian is a dead Indian."

Generally indigenous people as you encountered them were judged to be inferior, good--if good at all-- only in so far as they could be remade in the image of the invaders and made to perform useful tasks. Perhaps the most infamous statement expressing this point of view was that uttered by Captain Richard Henry Pratt regarding the purpose of Carlisle Indian Boarding School: "All the Indian there is in the race should be dead. Kill the Indian in him and save the man." Pratt's statement, though perhaps less repeated than Sheridan's, epitomizes the goals of Indian policy as it was practiced in the United States from his time through the present. To this end came multiple assimilation policies like allotment which meant to make of these "uncivilized" people farmers (and to relieve them of their "excess" land).

Most people can recognize these overt attacks on native culture for what they are. However, the autonomy of Native Americans continues to come under attack, and the uselessness or usefulness of Indian people remains a major part (although a frequently unrecognized part) of the rhetoric of all the would-be Indians experts, reformers and occupiers of tribal lands. And if you look carefully, Chris, you can see the ghosts of Darwinian debates about the stages of evolution and the status of native peoples lurking in the background in moves throughout the country to obtain mineral rights to tribal lands, in moves to deny tribal rights to hunt, fish and gather, and in moves to site nuclear waste repositories on tribal lands. It seems to me, Christopher, that the present battle in Wisconsin over spearfishing is merely a modern day version of an endless drama. It clearly has ties to the same politically motivated historical posturing, to the ideas of manifest destiny. Why should mere Indians (you know those sub-human savages) be allowed to take fish for food or as part of their livelihood when vacationers (those on the tip top of the human evolutionary ladder) could enjoy the recreation of fishing and the tourist industry could reap the financial benefits? Why haven't those redskins learned to perform more useful duties, after all they have all the benefit of the guidance of the Great White Father whose paternalism continues to operate so efficiently through the Bureau of Indian Affairs? After all weren't they given both the religious and the industrial education they needed in boarding schools and mission schools to become good citizens? Weren't they welcomed into factory jobs in major cities throughout the country courtesy of government relocation programs?

And, it seems to me, Chris, that the developers of twentieth century America have stolen a page or two of propaganda from the manifest destiny theory, learned well the skills of justification: How can you place the good of animals, plants, or any of those "things" of lesser value, they ask, before that of humankind? Expansion, they profess, is a right of the "chosen people" and a necessity. Why protect the spotted owl, for god's sake, when you have these people who need to make a living by cutting those trees? Both arguments--those for the taking of tribal lands and those for the "development and improvement" of wild areas--operate by privileging one group above another (colonizers above native peoples, expanding human population above all other living beings) and by claiming expansion as a necessity not simply as a desire. And so today, Christopher, the future of the indigenous peoples of Alaska, the natural creatures there, and the Alaskan eco-system are being weighed against the "need" for the barrels of oil that will keep the machinery of civilization moving forward. But will the matter be weighed on the scales of justice or will the story of Oklahoma oil exploitation be repeated?

Do you see how little has really changed, Christopher? Of your encounters with the islanders you wrote that you were "attentive and worked hard to know if there was any gold." The yellow gold that you sought has become the black gold of Beverly Hillbilly's fame, but the search is still for wealth and power and the method is still to devalue and destroy whatever might stand in the way. Thinking about this I find it absurd to believe that it is *American Indians* who are said to have no religion.

Of course, I admit, Chris, that I tend to find a great many events and ideas in the encounter between indigenous peoples and Europeans absurd, sometimes hilariously absurd, sometimes tragically. I mean don't you think it utterly incredible that the valuable time of a good many legal minds is spent battling tribal bingo? Really, Christopher--bingo, for god's sake. A Harvard education used to tighten drug laws and reduce gang violence? No. Used to prevent nuclear proliferation and work for strategies of world peace? No. Used instead to prevent tribes from earning too darn much money from bingo, to keep the gold in the hands of the conquerors. Absurd, right? And Chris, you will love this one. Remember how you were trying to find that route to China? Well guess where many of the "authentic" native crafts are made these days? Absolutely, absurdly true-- China! Take my word for it, the lengths of absurdity in Indian law and politics in the past 500 years is infinite.

One of my favorite stories and one of the most characteristic of the twentieth century absurdities, comes to me, Christopher, from a fine old gentleman from one of the Wisconsin tribes and involves that tribe's battle to gain the fishing fights guaranteed them in their treaty with the United States government. These rights had systematically been denied for years. For years this gentleman and his fellow tribal members would set nets for fish and would frequently be arrested by the Department of Natural Resources, have their equipment confiscated, go to court, be found guilty of violating state statutes, and pay a fine. "Every time I turned around," my storyteller professed, "I was getting arrested." Finally after certain landmark legal cases had found in favor of Native American tribes and upheld their treaty rights, this tribe, too, decided to challenge the law. But suddenly, Chris, they couldn't get arrested. "I tried for two years," the gentleman exclaims, "I couldn't get arrested!" So began an earnest campaign to accomplish what they had tried to avoid for years: to be arrested. The fishermen went so far as to put their names on their illegal nets. The nets would be found and confiscated, but no one came to charge them.

Finally an arrest was made and a target case wound its way through the court system. The tribe won. Their treaty rights were upheld. In an odd sort of compromise arrangement the waters were split into parcels with certain sections being tribal waters, certain public, and they were separated by imaginary lines of demarcation And so one morning my storyteller was out on the lake fishing when he was approached by another boat which held the game warden and he found himself accused: "You're fishing on the wrong side of that imaginary line," declared the game warden. "Well, god dammit," he replied in understandable frustration, "I imagine it's over here!" And this, Christopher, is a parable for our time. It might say that life is absurd and we shouldn't take it too seriously. It might say that if you are a Native American, you will always find yourself on the wrong side of that imaginary line. It might say it's time that Indian people began to imagine clearly their own lines, against all authority. Or it might be just a story that is told. But I believe it is true, Christopher. How about you?

When you look back, Christopher, I wonder if you find it heartening to see you have left a legacy so strong? Or can you see with longer vision from the bow of eternity? Do you watch in horror as your every error is enshrined in the history of Western civilization because you now see that each supposed conquest will turn back on itself at the expense of all life? I find it ironic and perhaps the last best absurdity that you, Christopher, who professed so vehemently that the world was round, should live so carelessly--as if the world were flat.

Sincerely,

Kimberly M. Blaeser
(Anishinabe)

Dear Christopher:

       I thought about writing you and your descendants a more elaborate letter, but I decided that I would not. Over the last six years in university I have written countless reports and even a thesis in the fashion which you and your descendants proscribe, so that my ideas can be understood by your population. I have had to chose my words carefully so as to not overly insult your population in the hopes that you would not only complete reading what I had written but might also think about it. I have had to censure words such as domination, genocide and racism so that I would not be classified as an irrational individual whose work must be ignored. This time I write for myself and I am sure you can learn to interpret, just as I have had to do.

The trees bend with the weight of snow
White shaded with grey and purple in the moonlight
I follow Father's footsteps deeper into the woods
He turns motioning me with silent lips to look at the ground
Footsteps of the doe and baby
Tracks leading further into the bush
       No sign of hurry
            No sign of fear
                  Of the white wolf
Protected under the blanket of the moon

Father's eyes are bright, content
They are as the stars above us in the dark night
No resemblance to the eyes that were full of
       confusion
           fear
               and unhappiness
When we lived in the wolf's den.

Dear Christopher

500 years of oppression
36 of them mine
    seem to disappear as I follow
      Father's footsteps
        still further into the bush
Turning a deaf ear to the baying of the wolf
In the far-away distant night
I am with, all my relation.

Sincerely,

Marcelle Gareau

Woman whose Father
named her
Pois-Plume
But known to you as
#018-0998

Dear Christopher:

Please excuse me if I do not come to your party. There has been a lot happening round here since you first arrived. It is not an easy matter, Chris, to look back twenty years ago or five hundred years ago and feel perfectly calm about what has transpired. Believe me, if human-kind could learn by its mistakes, we would all be saints, too cool and too perfect to melt in the sun. Yet, fools that we are, when we do look back we often search for extenuating circumstances.

Do you remember when you gave that order about everyone over fourteen years of age being required to bring in every three months so much gold? That edict must have caused a wide smile to appear on your soldier's faces. After-all, it sounded efficient enough: three months to scratch around for the precious metal, deliver the stuff, then back for more. Your men could go along with that, eh, Chris? And to show the little buggers that you meant business, you left those who did not meet their quota minus a pair of hands. The soldiers, of course, could say they were only carrying out orders.

How did it happen? You must have thought that you belonged to the only race of people who could be called people. That kind of thinking, I understand, was a problem back in those times. If they had had the weapons, wouldn't they have done it to you? Expediency. The old European know-how. The rabbits were created for hungry men. The sun rises and it sets; only those who survive will own the field. Some will go along with that. Today it is referred to as Mylai. But even then--and here comes another tough crew--there were objections from a few opinionated holy men, those who said much and did little, those who ate well and had, if St. Peter is honest, their share of mistakes. It was a raw and primitive world, no doubt about that. Any man who thought he was blameless, well, he never got off the boat.

But it is true that after vicissitudes and trials that a man does look back with regret, knowing that he might have accomplished more, or perhaps, walked at a different pace. The cost of arms he wears and the restless, lustful men who follow along speak persuasively, even in the stillness of night. So I was a man of my times. Is that so strange? Have I not stood long hours watching the sea? Yet, there were few who would venture forth, and of those few there were fewer yet with convictions. They had to be led. It was as simple as that.

So you are no doubt right to refuse to join it--it was, after all, a party of blood, at least in the beginning. You offer polite excuses. My New World friend, I will lose no sleep over that. Just as you can hardly see into your past years, so could I only dimly see what was ahead. The fat priests have at least one foot on the truth; there is a greater view of things that calls us from our dark little caves and hamlets. Who knows what it is? We only know we must be a-searching.

Consider the roar of a mighty river pouring forth from a green expanse of land. I know at last that this sound, this freshness, this ablution came from the very pure and holy breasts of Paradise. Because I had embarked on a strange and hazardous voyage, God permitted me, out of all my countrymen, to see this wondrous sight. This bold mariner put sacks of gold in the hands of a queen. Did she ask how many lives, how many agonized screams were also in these sacks? Monarchs and Gods reward those who serve. There were none who could tell me which direction to take, what forces would appear, what the nights would hold.

Be weak and indecisive--those were the big sins in my world, in spite of what the brown robes taught. But it is clear that no man in charge explains his world to another. Am I not a decrepit figure, an old World accident staggering down through the years? Am I not a rowdy ghost you future ones listen for and sometimes ridicule? So run ahead of me, if you can. A pox on you, if you try. But why do I waste my breath? I catch a scent of your foul existence, and, aye, the mighty oaks from within. I will not tickle your fancy by recounting your many failings, since you seem to delight in all manner of scandal and perversions. Your cities march back to the Dark Ages, your clergy are no more enlightened than ours, even with 2,000 years of reading. But continue on, pick up the rod, and say how will you seem to those who live 500 more years ahead. How will *they* see you? What, has the miserable cat got also your tongue? I, of course, will be there, but will you? Already, like some strange New World bird, you have fouled your nest thrice over. Answer! You are so great at unraveling conundrums and your own horde of gold.

You stand, I see, on your reputation, as do most of the pig-headed of the past. But if you think I am going to strut about like a gamecock for your amusement, you are vastly mistaken. It might be true that our ship of state is hardly more seaworthy than one of yours, but it has not gone down yet and there are some who give it credit, if not for good passage, at least for safe passage. As for your stinking priests, they are now almost as numerous as the lusty soldiers--if you can believe that. And that statement in itself says something about the voyage we are on. But, old Genocide, let's get down to particulars. We are both here, you might say, at the opposite ends of history. We can blow smoke and pretend, or we can make good use of the moment.

I speak, you see, as though I am a bona fide part of the system. If I can look at you and say that with a straight face, then you indeed should realize that you are out of it, the shadow of an Old World feather on the forest floor. Now, it may well be that I am the so-called marginal man, the fellow in the last house, the last to be invited anywhere, but I, too, have heard the Grandfather of all Waters and have inhaled the pure and holy air that moves outward from its banks. The vision of what might be is still--however the "what" is defined--a possibility. And some, like cattle nearing a stream, have caught the scent. The meatheads who turn their vision into rabbit stew, of course, are still problems. Are not these of little imagination always with us?

Therefore, going past Howth Castle and environs, I find that I am cut off at every turn. Yet, in the chill of the night I think at times that I am there, there at the crossing, there within sight of my destination. How great that is! There is music in the thought and not of one kind only but a grand rhythm and sometimes a crystal clarity. You know, freedom is hard to describe. It has a certain taste and how that fits in with the vision proper is difficult to say; yet, I am certain there is a connection.

You could not sail into the heartland, O heartless voyager, and you missed something there, I'll say that. The prairie grass is also like the sea. Too often the wretched cities grab us up, bind us like Odysseus to the mast, although we know that it's of our own doing. What siren song do we hear? What melodies are like knives in our chests? We often need to renew ourselves, return to those great open spaces, breathe again the mountain air. Could we hold freedom so dearly if those stretches of road were never there? I think not. There have to be places where nature itself holds sway, where man is the intruder, the unwelcome guest. In some places the mighty oak can still die in peace after a long and prosperous life. When the balance disappears, so will we.

The earliest people of my continent stood in awe of the heavens and the starry night. The great battles of the future may well be the subdued massive conflicts waged over the care and training of the human mind. Universal education has never set well in our troubled times. Those who are better prepared, I believe, will turn evermore to the skies, to that vision of final escape, to the search for privilege and privacy, while the center of our western world will perhaps move even further west, to the Orient or to the lands down under. Yes, you will be there, Senor Columb, but who will care? Very likely the earth itself will be on everyone's mind, for we also move through strange valleys of time. You challenge me to look forward, to step over the unborn tomorrows. Such predictions will always fail; yet, there are trends, or elephant-like prints in the earth, that one would be wise to notice.

If we move backward in time by 5,000 year increments, beginning with the year 2,000, it will take us but four large steps to reach an ice age in which a glacier-like shield stretched from the coasts of Washington to the shores of New York state. If we come forward again from 18,000 B.C., we find, according to the investigations of archaeology, that in 13,000 B.C. the deglaciation on the North American continent was evident and noticeable. In another 5,000 years there were definite archaeological signs of New World villages and burial sites. Beyond 8,000 B.C., that is, nothing is very definite about New World people. And in another 5,000 year step to 3,000 B.C., the land features as we know them in our time are established. The greatest change, as you will observe, has taken place in this last big step--to the year A.D. 2,000. This latter date is important because we are about to take another big stride into the unknown future and one in which the year A.D. 2492 is merely a drop in the bucket.

Sorry to bore you with numbers, Ghostly Mariner, but even the so-called scuzballs you wasted have now and then taken to bookish calculations. The elephant tracks show that the future will be difficult, even traumatic, but only on a scale that the far-sighted are able to deal with. But hasn't that always been so--on that point we don't pull the wool over your eyes. Look up at the stars. You are probably saying, "What in the hell are you waiting for?"

Good question. We are probably waiting for Mother Nature to give us a good boot in the slats. Within the next thousand years she is likely to do so. And, as you know, she can be pretty persuasive.

So, Ancient Sailor, others no doubt will rake you over the coals, but time is far too short for me to beat my chest on your account. In fact, it has been stimulating conversing with you, because, in truth, you have nothing to do with our present problems. Have you heard of a church social, gay rights, a town meeting, a tax write-off, the Third Reich, corn flakes, a Mac Computer, a light bulb, flu shots, a commercial for candy bars, the quality of life, post-modernism, diet soda pop, the Doppler effect, a Bach fugue, a Paul Klee painting, the Ghost Dance, visiting rights and alimony? In the next 500 years we no doubt will appear like so many Druids carrying sprigs of mistletoe around Stonehenge. But throw the dice--let the little bones talk. Here's a poem and another city beside the sea. I put you in it to create a certain effect. It's this vision thing again it's the one element that seems to span the years. Here it is.

*　　*　　*　　*

Freshly scented Pacific air, and spilling
over from ocean crests into Santa Barbara,
the perpetual whispers of the big sea.

Business types on the incoming plane,
mature, interested faces bending close
as driver spoke of murals somewhere,
gardens.

Dear Christopher

That exchange was thirty, thirty-two years
ago:
social ours in the cup passed noisily
from hand to hand. In the resort lobby

One evening the bellhop said, breathless-
like
"He's in the lounge right now. If you, well,
hurry." One of his idols, you see, had
arrived.

Who could it be, this person with verve and
dash?
In movies he was Jason, Hercules.
But my interests even then ran more

To pedestrian fare. Early morning scenes,
lights on the ocean points and a jogger
making his way along the ocean sand.

In daytime the conference and a trip
to our botanical garden: better,
you know, if you can manage

A lively friend or two; and a catalog
of survivors from green antiquity.
That day the two of them knew Latin
names,

So the hour turned upon gentle words
and fragrances as we strolled down the
path,
stopping the longest, I believe, at the mallow

Family (*Hibiscus syriacus*) before going on.
The greenery, I suppose, is thriving yet,
each year becoming fresh and young. That
thought

Was not there among the leaves or petals
then:
only upon reflection are the tables turned
as the breeze moves in from the western
sea;

Columbus, then, as a beachcomber,
wondering
what was beyond. Through the tangled
vines
and Old World forms, the view once again
was

Of murals--cannibals in a garden, well,
what else? The beginning of projects
moving at last off dead center? Daywatch?

So the Rose of Sharon has meaning now
as lightning in the hills again and rain-
laden clouds arise, although at times

It seems not so important to respond, for
Ninevah, like a cauldron of pointless days,
speaks of more of the same and appetite.

Finding the sun calendar, finding truth
in the labyrinth, tracking the eye
of the storm, watching--what else can we
do?

*   *   *   *

By the way, we will be here the next time around
and every bit as difficult to dispose of or overlook.
Because history, for its part, seems to concern itself
mainly with tyrants and madmen, the sitting ducks never
qualify for many words of encouragement. But we keep

coming on and very likely will continue to do so. On the other hand, Man of Genos, you have made your mark. You can proudly and complacently make your way down the bitter trails of the past and into the future. Let us pray God that we hold fast to the long range view and to decisions that permit the earth and all people living on it to grow and prosper. *Hasta la vista, Cristoforo Columbo.* The final lines of the good voyage have yet to be drawn.

Sincerely,

Charles G. Ballard
(Quapaw/Cherokee)

Dear Christopher:

Congratulations on your arduous task in successfully completing the trans-Atlantic journey. The hardships 500 years ago must have been taxing and, at the same time, exciting at the prospect of new adventures. It must have been a shock, especially for your fellow travellers who traversed over what is now termed North, Central, and South America, to see other people who actually had their own governments and distinct styles. And...to top it off, these new people had family structures, industries, and social organizations. Chris, it must have been quite a surprise to find thousands who could live without the rigors of constant wars raging back in Spain and Italy. These new people whom you name "Indians" (another blunder) could actually communicate with one another. This short letter is to remind you, had you stayed and really got to know these "Indians," you may have learned that they knew how to paint and sculpt (not scalp...that's your "contribution" to civilization), make all sorts of beautiful pottery and farm implements and, when needed, could actually sail the same waters you navigated (maybe not the distance, but at least along the coastal waterways). You do realize you missed seeing a multitude of native communities, especially in North America, where there were orderly societies (one still exists in northeaster Arizona). It's a shame you didn't stay, although I understand your sponsors had a final reward for your efforts...disgrace for all of your dreams. Many of the villages you failed to note not only contained strong family and religious structures but also complete irrigation systems and large-scale agricultural industries with tool making by skilled craftsmen.

At least, if you had remained here, this would have been a more productive life; you could never tell...you may have liked it. Moreover, you would be with honest people and while we were not "blessed" with religious wars, plagues, and economic disasters, you may have found a nice job building ships. Certainly, the lands provided all the resources you needed. The natives were healthy, friendly, and energetic. And, as time passed, you would have recognized that the inhabitants you met could be downright helpful and literate. But, unfortunately after you left, others came and blighted the land and exterminated a large percentage of its people. Someday, Chris, there may be a recognition that native people, especially in these lands, no matter how strange they appear, do have values and rights that just can't be eradicated if they don't fit in with a king's or religious concept's of one's philosophy of life. I hope someday, if your ancestors ever decide to come again, they will come with open minds and recognize that others do have their own culture and heritage, however strange the appearance, that do contain intrinsic beauty to be preserved and accepted.

Sincerely,

Karl E. Gilmont
aka
Charlie Gold Mountain
(Coharie)

Dear Christopher:

Who are you? A human hero ...NO. A greedy violent explorer? The father of slavery? The father of colonialism? ...MAYBE. Most historians have been a little rough on you, but popular press, especially Hollywood, has been reasonably kind (especially up until the past few years). Most elementary school teachers talk of you as a hero each October. Most residents of the U.S.A. think of your Monday holiday merely as a no mail/no bank day.

What did you, the Admiral of the Ocean sea, cause? Causality is a difficult term; cause and effect are often not provable; but consequences, whether intended or unintended, are real and the results do have impacts. Mr. Grand Admiral, let me report to you about a few of the consequences--some intended, some not. My tribe's ancestors experienced suffering ranging from mild harassment to violent murder, movement-immigration-relocation (whatever term used the result is the same) from Indiana to Kansas then to Indian Territory. My great-grandmother was allotted land in what is now Oklahoma and strongly encouraged to follow the ways (language and lifestyle) dictated by the White leadership. My grandfather attended Indian boarding schools as part of the assimilation process. Over the past 200 odd years my people have dealt with a wide array of official and de facto U.S. government policy--termination, removal, sovereignty, self-determination, acculturation, broken treaties, rigorous controls and regulation, and inconsistencies. Now in 1992 we are still dealing with continuing cliches.

Where do my tribe and others stand today? Uncertainty among an array of economic issues--land rights and usage, health care, education, tribal governance, business enterprise (is bingo really the new cash crop?) and economic development, and self-sufficiency. Yes, Viceroy Columbus, these certainly are important issues of our time. But, the issues that mean the most to me personally deal with CULTURE. For my tribe and most of the other 286 federally-recognized (just in the 48 contiguous states alone, not including Alaska, Canada, Mexico, and all areas to the south) and many non-recognized tribes, the substantial and in some cases complete loss of language, customs, rites, rituals, ceremonies, and basic way of life are gone. Yes, Governor General of the Islands, I said GONE...this is a consequence that is a fact, one that can't be corrected. The historical information about our past simply does not exist. While there are a few written and oral accounts of history about my tribe and others, there exists a great vacuum of facts (even folklore) about our native culture

The facts in 1992 that may seem to matter for most Native Americans is that we live in a very large place. The U.S.A. is large in population, area, and economic power. We of native blood are all-too-often not noticed. In spite of the movement over the past decade in the direction of greater diversity and cultural freedom, we have not yet achieved "perestroika". Most U.S. citizens spend very little time thinking about the Native Americans, and most of that very little time goes to bingo, hunting and fishing rights, convenience stores and smoke shops, and powwows/arts and crafts.

The Christopher Columbus Quincentary Jubilee Commission formally began its planning in 1984 for a "celebration throughout 1992". By the time this letter is published, many of those events will have occurred. While it could be unequivocally argued that we the indigenous Native Americans have been victimized with slavery, conquest, disease, and humiliation, I hope and think that the hoopla and splendor won't be too great and that many U.S. residents will spend some time recollecting about the great losses of culture that have resulted as the consequence of your activities, Mr. Christopher Columbus.

Sincerely,

Joseph W. Leonard
(Miami)

Dear Christopher:

I really don't blame you. I know that many folks do, many of my friends and family, and I know that pointing the symbolic finger of blame your way is the "correct" thing to do just now, particularly just now. Still, I can't blame you, but I can't really forgive you either; that would be a bit too much, even for me.

You see, I know that you were of your time and place--just like me. Well, not exactly, but the forces that shaped and propelled you must have been just as compelling, just as apparently right and good, as those that filled my own sails, blowing some forty years ago back in Fort Smith, Arkansas. Like you, I went out on a voyage into the unknown, the uncharted, with mythic beasts abounding, filled with conviction and a desire for more and better--what?--and like you, I didn't know what I'd find, or that my terminus really wouldn't be mine alone to claim, or that some really good people would get hurt in the process. All accident, not much real meanness. But brother, we both have to take responsibility for what we became and what we set in motion.

You need to understand where I came from, the land and the attitude (I know this isn't very comforting, but it's about all we've got to hold onto, an understanding, an awareness, a truth). Born and raised across the river from Indian Territory, I was fourth generation semi-urban, blessed (perhaps) with a comfortable, upwardly mobile, middle-class family, emerging into a town and a set of expectations not of my choosing. Like your youth, mine was a time of transitions, movements, potential--if only I were bold enough, nothing stood in my way.

Actually, one thing did loom in the near distance, following me like it had my father, and his, and his before him. Indian blood. Lots of it, and drawn from a bunch of folks around my town, a white island in a red sea. In hushed tones and euphemisms, my grandmother let me know I was a sort of mongrel--Cherokee was OK, if the blood was old and minimal, but Choctaws were unattractive, and who ever had heard of a beautiful Quapaw princess, and, of course, those Shawnees were just oil-rich trash. You need to know this, she said, but don't talk about it; after all, and most importantly, I could PASS. Thanks be to great-grandmaw Jonnie, Tom Collins' Irish second wife. Those Celtic genes were powerful (medicine?), throwing one fair-skinned blond each generation, this time me, lucky me. This was my very own PASS.

So it was mostly circumstance, quirky biology that allowed me to ignore biological realities. Like you, in a certain place at a certain time with a special and rare chance and someone urging me on. Who could blame me? Or you?

So I set forth, only a little Cherokee, safely distant and faintly exotic, to recreate myself, a pampered, Protestant White boy. My grandmother didn't really approve of my spending most of my time alone in the woods, in the hills and into the Ozarks, but few knew and social acceptance came my way easily, looking and behaving as I did, as I was pointed. Her memory failed exponentially, however, when I asked questions about my grandfather, dead before I was born, whom she had married twice (her own special skeleton). He was wild, an enchanter, she said; all the girls followed the flag of his red hair as he roared through the 1920s in our town. But Big Houston came to no good, drank himself to death. Bad blood. But not in me. Finally, no one could remember him, or his daddy, not even my daddy. The past is buried, somewhere, and the future is the undiscovered country.

After a time in this place, I set out like you did, further from him, further from those circling Indians, more pale successes promising equally more potential. The last stage, the last stamp on my PASS, came in my 21st year. A college degree in hand, I had proven worthy to be freed from that last flaw, that last bothersome (if not quite telling) mark of my burdensome heritage: with my nose reshaped and my cheekbones smoothed over, I was now fully homogenized, fully freed of the past--at least to the eye, if not to the eye that sees within to the core of our being.

(My shame is now just how plastic I was, how much I allowed others to shape me--quite literally. What was my passport has become my mark of dishonor. How little we know of the malign consequences of our intentions!)

Whiter now than ever, I was granted the luxury that four generations before me had planned for; I could avoid the inevitable conflict with a hostile culture and "regret"-- wanting nothing, I set sail for Ph.D., the next port on my voyage. I could become a certified, card-carrying intellectual (no DIBs or tribal enrollments in that boy's wallet, no sir). This was the symbolic new world in my family's eyes, transfixed with appearances, with marks of acceptance in a world closed to them--until now.

Outside, I grew blonder, more professorial, and inside questions began. My training afforded access to information and I had all the skills to discover what had been hidden, by both time and will. And my training afforded me a capacity for understanding, even empathy. For my own sake, I explored toward the edges, somehow sensing the existence of a circle in my own terra incognita. I wanted to find out if the bits I remembered in my blood were just romantic nonsense (Vine Deloria, Jr., told me as I read more and more that everyone claimed a Cherokee grandmother and he, for one, was tired of the hypocrisy and nonsense). And no one believed me when I spoke of my fathers, giggling and pointing to my hair, to my green eyes. I wasn't sure I believed in me, anymore.

For two long and frustrating years I explored, thought to be more than a bit odd by those who witnessed my departure. But I finally did arrive, and what I discovered was myself. Finally, I met my fathers, seeing them for really who they were, and are still yet in me. My carefully planned and imposed line straight up and out had looped back, forming a circle, closing the hoop in my head. I exchanged my PASS for my tribal enrollment card, my new and true passport.

Some folks still scoff, but few now doubt my reality, my re-discovered land inside, my sincerity. Like you, I traveled far to "discover" what many before me knew full well, and I didn't have to take anything by force; my place waited for me all along, for four generations, in the very land I had left (I bet you were relieved to get back home, too). Still, some were hurt along the journey; some of my family feel betrayed, deceived. Some feel shame, a secret foolishly revealed, long-held goals thrown overboard. Some blame me for what I did, just like some blame you.

But you understand, coming from your particular place in your particular time. No other route but the dangerous and improbable was available. We did what we inevitably had to do.

We both found Indians, me within and you without, and I guess that's where our courses take different directions. Now, in this time in this place, I must work to help restore some measure of that which you inadvertently changed forever. My Ph.D. can now be a tool for, rather than against, my people. And I can't blame you for your voyage into the unknown. Neither of us found quite what we expected, and what we found wasn't all ease and benevolence, but each of us must find out what *really* is out (or in) there--must understand truths, however difficult, and accept the responsibility for our quests.

I have returned home, dear Christopher, and you are partly to blame and to thank. But I wanted to let you know--I understand how difficult things must be for you right now--we are brothers in many ways, all of us.

Sincerely (nvwhtohiyada),

Rodney Simard
(Cherokee)

Dear Christopher:

THREE BULLS VIEWS THE PORTRAIT OF COLUMBUS

Did they tell you they had waited it out
in shelter unsafe for winds from the east?
That the wooden framing strained like your boats'
and that this unheard of storm from the sea

ripped the door from their hiding,
took it away and they ran for the trees?
Were they blinded by sparks from blowing fire
while they shivered and slept in the open?

The next morning I imagine your boats
already there, their arrival a scar,
halfwit platoons to die at your word, devils
drawing lines round themselves on the beaches.

No mere rain could wash that clay smile as
following tales of resurrection
you carried your will sovereign halfway
round the earth, teasing out jewels from crowns.

Could they imagine what it was you brought,
the sheer crush of everything needed
for getting here and getting back again
and making *here* seem like *there*, and returning,

and the torch that you put to the forest
and the plow that you pushed through the prairie
and the steel that you put in the breast,
grandfathers melting away in the gale,

led to Gould and to Frick and these houses,

Dear Christopher

where soft chairs turned from last year's
   paintings
to face this year's newest old masters, that
these buttons pressed could call Irish servants?

Swords carried like crosses down streets of flame
made easy the warm dreaming parlors.
and kneeling nations behind rose windows
forgot jimpson weed and sycamore leaves,

made the earth unendurable
and morning sky a hemorrhage of red.

Where they once sat now we all stand
   with tapes, hats, furs before pictures gilt-framed
and
   hung there by builders, explorers, and thieves
   separate from what we might love
   by all that we think we have.

   Sincerely,

   John W. Presley
   (Choctaw)

Dear Christopher:

Surprisingly, hundreds of years after your death, I have been asked to write you a letter from the heart about your expeditionary misdeeds and their aftermath in the western hemisphere. I have agreed to this task. Realistically, however, you cannot receive a letter at your abode in Hell, although spiritually you may receive a message there, providing your Keeper lets it through. Therefore on this plane I shall dwell briefly, empowered to communicate these words to you.

To begin, never expect forgetfulness on my part, only forgiveness, perhaps. After all, your willfulness and its consequent evil-doings remain alive in your followers. Ignoring history, they also continue ignorantly, slavishly, and wrongheadedly to esteem your efforts as a discoverer and thereupon raise you to the status of historical hero, when in fact as a villain you killed people, misnamed their survivors, destroyed property, trespassed, and then surely lied about it all to save your temporal skin. Thus the record damns you, while your followers persistently err, doubly hampering forgiveness.

Nonetheless, I forgive you, on these conditions, that you make a nonstop effort to dispel your personal ignorance, that you always set the record straight whenever presented with the opportunity, and that you do your utmost to attain purity of thought and action by applied gnosis. Fulfilling these requirements may prove difficult in your pinching circumstance, owing to distraction by repeated suffering and to absence of a modern library. So I hereby offer you these pointers.

Abandon the notion that you discovered anything. You merely found for yourself and your kin a land already inhabited since time immemorial by a diverse, unique people. In fact, by the informed standard of today you may claim no title greater than explorer. Foreswear all other titularity. Doing so will reduce falsehood and serve accuracy. Perpetuating by allowing an untrue status for yourself presents an obstacle to forgiveness.

Admit completely the now-undeniable fact that you misnamed the people with whom you came in contact, by calling them "Indians" after the Asians you had expected to encounter. The native peoples of the lands on which you set foot each had a distinctive name. By lumping them under the misnomer "Indians," you started a distortive process we nowadays term "stereotyping." This simplism denudes the aboriginal peoples of their evolved uniqueness, as well as their diversity, which together remain unexampled anywhere. You must confess to this antisocial behavior without an iota of lukewarmness, but instead with a wholehearted effort. Then you must learn and use the proper names. Thus you may gain an easy credit toward forgiveness.

Open your eyes, heart, and mind to perceive the discoloring on your hands as bloodstains from murdering the original inhabitants of the lands onto which you stumbled. Being your worst crime, this killing foreshadowed more of the same to follow. As history records, your brethren, the Europeans, saw fit to practice genocide on the various peoples they met here. (By the way, this word "genocide," coined in our time, means, "the deliberate and systematic destruction of a racial, political, or cultural group.") In view of the awful magnitude of this villainy and your setting the stage by example for its continuance, to win forgiveness of it becomes almost insurmountably difficult to achieve. Know, however, that if you turn unswervingly to your own heart, with a mind to cleanse it, you will thereby at least set yourself on the right path. You may become a regenerate.

Your Keeper has just appeared and cut short our communication. He grants a moment to say good-bye. I wish you well, and salute any effort you may undertake to correct yourself.

Sincerely,

Ed Burbee
(Luiseño)

PS. If this little afterword reaches you, say hello to Padre Junipero Serra. You should find him residing in your locality, for he committed crimes similar to yours. He arrived there about 200 years ago. Identify him also by hands discolored from bloodstains in his killing of native peoples wholesale. He too will learn deliverance from his torment to be most difficult, for the same reason you will, but especially so because his earthly supporter, the Catholic Church, arrogantly blinding itself to the oral history of native peoples telling of his genocide, proposes to elevate him to sainthood. Hence this act, by its disregard, will only intensify his unholiness, and not subtract one instant from his suffering. Hard words these are, yes, but true. For liberation he must likewise clear his ignorance, renounce unearned titles, diligently rectify the historical record, and mindfully purify his heart. No proxy religious effort will suffice. He alone must purge himself of sins against mankind. Enough. Our visit ends. Good-bye and good luck, to both of you.

Dear Christopher:

Columbus
The Myth and the Man

Five hundred years after the arrival of Christopher Columbus in the New World, the Indians are everywhere in America the poorest of the poor and the least powerful of all groups. Future generations, however, may look back on the 20th Century as the turning point in the struggle for Indian autonomy and powers in the Americas.

Perhaps no figure in the history of the world has been surrounded by more carefully cultivated myths than Christopher Columbus. The following is intended as a handy guide for debunking key elements of this mythology among students, grades 1-12. Unfortunately, it may be equally applicable for educational use at the college level, in offices inhabited by the staff of National Endowment for the humanities, and other "intellectually mature" circles.

Fiction: Columbus was from the city of Genoa, and was therefore Italian.

Fact: There is no conclusive evidence of this.

Fiction: Columbus was actually Spanish.

Fact: A group of 20th century Spanish "scholars" forged supposedly "proving" Columbus' Spanish origins. The hoax has been exposed.

Fiction: Columbus was secretly a Jew who had converted to Christianity.

Fact: There is no solid proof of this either. In reality, no one knows who Columbus was. Hence, no nation or ethnicity can advance a bona fide "claim" to him.

Fiction:Columbus died a wealthy hero of Spain.

Fact: Coluumbus died a discredited pauper who was considered a criminal by his former employer, the Crown of Spain.

Fiction: Columbus "discovered" America in 1492.

Fact: America has been continuously occupied for at least 40,000 years. There were as many as 120 million people already living in this hemisphere when he arrived. It is impossible to discover a place which is already inhabited.

Fiction: Columbus was, as Samuel Eliot Morrison put it, one of history's greatest navigators.

Fact: When he landed in Espanola, Columbus believed he had reached the islands of the Asian subcontinent, halfway around the world. One can't be more lost than that!

Fiction: As a consequence of his navigational error, Columbus "mistakenly" described New World natives as "Indians."

Fact: Columbus was looking for a new route to what was then called Hindustan. Hindustan was not renamed "India"--by the British, not the Spanish--for another century and a half. The term "Indian," as Columbus applied it to the New World population, is from the Italian "In Dios," meaning "People of God." The description was no mistake.

Fiction: Columbus was concerned with the spice trade and was therefore seeking a short route to Asia in order to make imports of nutmeg, cinnamon and tea more efficient and profitable.

Fact: Columbus was a *slave* trader along the west coast of Africa prior to his 1492 voyage. The first "resource" he brought back from Espanola was a group of Indians to be sold as slaves in Spain.

Fiction: Columbus didn't really participate in the vast atrocities which followed his landing on Espanola.

Fact: Columbus returned to the island as its governor in 1492-3, a position he held for nearly a decade. By the time of his departure, he had implemented policies of slavery and extermination which led to reduction of the indigenous Taino people from as many as 8 million in 1492 to about 24,000 in 1524. His regime thus served as a model for all the horrors perpetrated by the Spanish in the centuries ahead.

Fiction: Whatever his motivations and defects, Columbus introduced civilization to the New World.

Fact: Civilization means "to live in cities." The great cities of the Aztecs, Mayas, and Incas equalled, and in some ways surpassed, anything created by the Europeans of Columbus' day. In North America, the single city of Cahokia had long-since attained a population of about 40,000. The European immigrants are also credited with carving out "civilition," as roads and townsites, from a "wilderness," when the fact of the matter is that these "boat people" built on top of already existing indigenous roadways, some of them grand highways, and villages or pueblos, even city-state empires. As an illustration, the site of Washington, D.C. is often cited as a pioneer example, as the nation's capitol, when it was actually built on an Indian village after the native people had been massacred by the colonists.

Fiction: Columbus brought concepts of enlightened government to the New World.

Fact: At the point of the Columbian "discovery" New World peoples such as the Iroquois and Creel confederacies were practicing highly sophisticated forms of democracy. Europe, by contrast was governed--and would continue to be for two centuries and more--by a system of feudal monarchy. American Indians enlightened European concepts of governance, not the other way around.

Fiction: If not governance, then the Columbian forays ushered in notions of enlightened jurisprudence.

Fact: Native American exhibited no appreciable criminal behaviour such as theft, assault, rape or murder during pre-Columbian times. On the rare occasions when such behavior was manifested, it was handled without recourse to institutionalized courts or jails and prisons. Europe, for its part, relied upon such refined "juridical methods" such as the "trial by fire" (A suspect was deliberately burned. If he or she blistered as a result, s/he was pronounced guilty and executed by such delicate methods as beheading or burning at the stake.)

Fiction: When Columbus first encountered them, the indigenous inhabitants of the New World were in a state of savagery marked by primitive superstition and cannibalism.

Fact: Although Columbus wrote in his journal of hearing that peoples such as the Caribs were cannibals, neither he nor anyone else seems ever to have found proof of this. Indeed, there is no hard evidence that *any* Native American people *ever* practiced cannibalism. Columbus' own Christian tradition, on the other hand, practiced (and still does) ritual cannibalism as a matter of course. This occurs during what is called "communion" when participants eat little wafers symbolizing Christ's flesh and drink wine symbolizing Christ's blood.

Fiction: Columbus' expedition brought agriculture to the "hunter-gatherer" peoples of the New World.

Fact: About two-thirds of all the vegetal foodstuffs commonly consumed by people around the world today were under cultivation in America--and nowhere else--at the point of Columbus' arrival. This included corn, potatoes, tomatoes, peppers, most beans, squash. The Europeans of Columbus' day were much more dependent for survival upon gathering fish from the sea, etc., than were American Indians. Put another way, the peoples of the New World were far more advanced agriculturally than were the hunter-gatherers of 15th century Spain, France and England.

Fiction: There were no real concepts of science or mathematics in America before Columbus came.

Fact: Actually, the Mesoamerican civilizations had a knowledge of astronomy far more refined than did Europeans. The Aztec calendar was projected five centuries into the future with seven decimal points greater degree of accuracy than Europe's Julian calendar. The Mayas invented the concept of zero, and were manipulating nine digit numbers by 1400. European mathematics did not begin to equal indigenous American systems for nearly four centuries after Columbus, and in some ways has yet to catch up.

Fiction: Columbus at least brought along advanced concepts of medicine which were of benefit to American Indians.

Fact: Native people in American had perfected the world's most sophisticated system of pharmacology long before Columbus arrived. The Incas, among others, were practicing successful brain and eye surgery, and had invented syringes and other surgical tools for such purposes. By comparing, European doctors were still involved with applying leeches to patients in order to draw of the "bad blood" imagined to cause their illnesses.

Fiction: Columbus and his men introduced concepts of hygiene and sanitation to the "dirty" Indians.

Fact: Unlike their American Indian counterparts across the Atlantic, denizens of European cities habitually dumped their sewage and other refuse into the streets. The "Black Death" and other epidemic diseases which reduced Europe's population by millions in the decades prior to Columbus' voyages were brought on primarily by the filth and squalor sin which most Europeans lived. In most European societies of Columbus' day--and for a long time thereafter--the simple act of bathing was considered a criminal offense (Queen Elizabeth I of England, for example, is reputed *never* to have bathed). One native "superstition" European explorers found most offensive was a tendency to bathe daily.

Fiction: Columbus, or his society, introduced beneficial ideas and processes like the wheel and metallurgy to Indians.

Fact: The wheel had been known in the New World for centuries before Columbus, as is evidenced by an abundance of wheeled toys among the Incas, Mayas, Aztecx and others. The Spaniards learned high altitude metallurgical procedures from the Incas.

Fiction: Whatever else may be said, Columbus and his friends did introduce *some* things to the New World which yielded a significant impact.

Fact: This is actually true. The "things" in question include diseases like measles, mumps, the common cold, influenza, diptheria, typhoid, whooping cough, the plague, typhus, and various venereal diseases, as well as substances like distilled spirits and concepts such as "the divine right of kings" and wars of annihilation.

Fiction: It is, as historian William Axtell claims, "unfair and misleading" to compare Columbus and the Columbian legacy to nazis and nazism.

Fact: This is probably also true. After all, nazism was rather short-lived, while the enterprise launched by Columbus has lasted centuries and is ongoing. Again, the nazis were able to exterminate about 75% of all Jews and Gypsies within their reach (as well as a few million Slavs, Poles and other "undesirables") while the Columbian legacy yielded an approximate 98% liquidation of Native North Americans by 1890. The nazis may ultimately have been responsible for the deaths of 40 million people. Columbus and his heirs have tallied several hundred million over the years and are still counting. Thus, bad as nazism was (and it was absolutely, unequivocally horrible) the process associated with Columbus' name has been--documentably and quantifiably--far, far worse.

Ultimately, there is much to be gained in realizing, as the historian Jack Weatherford already has, the simple truth that, "The Indian civilizations crumbled in the face of the Old World not because of any intellectual or cultural inferiority. They simply succumbed in the face of disease and brute strength. While the American Indians had spent a millenia becoming the world's greatest farmers and pharmacologists, the people of the Old World spent a similar period amassing the world's greatest arsenal of weapons. The strongest, but not necessarily the most creative or the intelligent, won the day." The brief recasting of data which appears above - offered not in a spirit of achieving "political correctitude" (whatever *that* is), but in recognition of our mutual and elemental need for accuracy in understanding our collective past - should provide an informational basis from which anyone can begin the necessary process of rethinking the meaning of Columbus and the resulting nature of the society in which we now live.

Sincerely,

M. Annette Jaimes
(Juaneño/Yaqui)

Dear Christopher:

In 1492
Columbus sailed the ocean blue
planted the seed of greed
called The People red

In 1992
Columbus is dead
The people endure____nuff' said.

      Sincerely,

      Yvonne Metivier
      (Oneida)

Dear Christopher:

My name is Peter David. I was born at Allakaket, Alaska, in the year of 49, August 15. I am half Koyukon Athabascan Indian and half Inupaiq Eskimo. Also, I am a full time student at the University Of Alaska, Fairbanks Campus. Majoring in the Human Service Technology, hopefully to become a substance abuse counselor.

I was doing okay in my classes here at the university. I was happy and very well situated, understanding that all I had to do was attend classes and do my homework. And then Bam! I was hit with something that I could not understand.

Your name popped out in one of my classes. I drew a blank, I did not know that you existed until now. I had to write this letter to you or else fail. All I wanted to do was learn to write stories of my past experiences. All of a sudden I was real mad. I could not come up with anything good to say about you, when they say that you discovered America.

Then this funny feeling was inside of my body. I had to come up with something to write. I threw this around for about one week and a half. Still I had nothing to write.

Again I thought of my ancestors--of how they were treated by the dominating culture--how they lost their lands and several tribes wiped-out of this world.

Why did all of these bad experiences happen?

As I stand today and look upon the land that my great-grandfathers have seen, (it is still the way it was when the day you are said to have discovered America), I see the same mountains and hills. When I go out in the country where my grandfathers walk, they are with me.

I could feel their presence by the wind in my face or by the firelight at night. This I thought to myself is how my great-grandfathers might have felt at one time--how much they loved their land and the people they walked with. As I sat there by the fire at night I had nothing to fear. My grandfathers told me that when you have a small fire burning and you are alone, that animals will not come up to the fire.

I always wondered, what was it like to be out and hear noise out in the dark. Is it an animal or is it a whiteman? These feelings I will never know. I feel sad and at peace when I sit there. Without them, I would not be here. This thought is always on my mind.

Listen Christopher. Listen to the wind in the tree tops. Listen to the fire crackling, and the picture in your mind of the firelight dancing on your brother's smiling face. Is that not freedom and peace to all good men? Did you ever have this feelings at one time or another, Christopher? I believe you did not.

All the sickness and disease the whiteman have given to us, we will survive. And all the evil and bad things they have done to our people, they will be forgiven so that our great-grandfathers can rest in peace. They can go to the Great Spirit in the Sky and show us where we will meet again. You can have your day, Christopher, for your own people.

Then again coming back to reality, I would say "basi" Ana "basi". (Thank You, in the Athabascan language.)

Listening to the fire and wind in the tree tops sends a charge through my spine. It made me sit straighter and I felt my scalp moved. This I understand as my worries and fears were being lifted.

I could see the plains where the buffalo roamed. As far as the eye could see, this land was made to be free. My brothers to the south riding their fine ponies with bowstrings pulled back to the tip of the arrow, knowing that they would have fresh meat for supper that night. Their families would have a great feast and the braves would be proud of who they are. The little ones would be playing, laughing and rolling around on the ground, pointing their fingers as make-believe weapons like their fathers when hunting.

They would hold this gathering into the night, and rest through out the next day with nothing to worry about. They were the people of the Great Land which gave them life year after year. They learned to live with the earth and would always know where they come from. Then giving thanks for who they are, they would then know where they are going.

Mr. Columbus, your people can do whatever with your day. My brothers and sisters will pray to our great-grandfathers, so that all the people of this world will unite and live under one law.

Instead of having Columbus Day. We should have a "New World Law Day."
Each culture celebrating its own beliefs.
Rest in Peace Mr. Columbus.
Your time is up. You can go now.
Good-bye.

Sincerely,

Peter David
(Athabascan/Inupaiq)

Dear Christopher:

My name is Samantha Whitefeather. I'm Anishinabeque, or Chippewa, and I'm 12 years old.

Many people think of you as a hero. I do not.
Many people honor you to this very day. I do not.
Many people think you discovered my homeland.
Once again, I do not.

Many people don't believe you were a cruel, greedy man. I do.
Many people don't believe you ever forced the native people to find
you gold. I do.
Many people don't know what kind of person you really were...I do.

People celebrate the day you landed on our shores.
Thinking you were in India, you mistakenly called the people
living here Indians. You made them find you gold, and if they didn't,
you cut off their hands. They bled to death.
Tell me why should we celebrate this day!?
Why should we celebrate the deaths of so many people?

I cannot change the past, but I can have enough sense to know
what really happened, and try to change the future.

    Sincerely,

    Samantha Whitefeather
    (Anishinabe)

Dear Christopher:

In the summer of 1492 as you set sail across the Atlantic seeking a western trade route to the Indies for the Spanish crown, you could not have anticipated the profound impact that your journey would have on millions of people around the world for centuries to come. Five hundred years after your precarious voyage we are still experiencing the repercussions of the contact between Western European cultures and the Indigenous cultures of the New World.

Five hundred years ago the world as you knew it was well defined by strict eschatological religious dogma. According to this world view there was no room for doubt or free thought. Any attempts to understand other cultural and religious systems were not necessary, since your culture had the only true interpretation of the natural and supernatural world. With the self-assured certainty that there was only one way to understand the world and that the purpose of life was only to test one's worthiness for an afterlife, the Spanish set out on a savage campaign of conquest and persecution of other cultures.

The year 1492 began with the Catholic conquest of Muslim Spain and continued with the expulsion of Jews from Spain. Without any regard for Muslim guardianship of classical knowledge during the European Dark Ages or their tolerance of Jews and Christians, the Spanish crown forbade the practice of Islam. The inquisition would continue the persecution of Jews and Muslims for decades to follow. How easy it must have been to have lived in a world in which one knew with certainty that his beliefs were the only correct ones and that all others were the work of the devil. It is at this time of extreme intolerance that you would begin your voyage.

Sailing west you eventually encountered occupied islands and called the inhabitants "Indians", thinking that you were off the coast of India. For years people would continue thinking that these islands were somewhere off the coast of Asia. For all practical purposes you might as well have been in Asia, since your cultural perspective could not allow you to comprehend alternative world views of any other cultures. The "Indian" cultures were equally exotic as any of those that you had heard of in Asia and would also be judged as equally inferior to the true Catholic European civilization. The actual colonization of Asia by "superior" Europeans will be postponed for decades after Europeans realize that you made contact with a "New World" which they will call "America" and make their target of colonization.

Continuing the pattern of religious intolerance and warfare in the conquest of Spain, Spanish conquistadores came to the New World and glorified their conquests as spreading the "true religion". Native cultures were easily dismissed as heathen savages. Today it is difficult for us to understand how one could have ordered the execution and enslavement of other people without any feelings of compassion or remorse. How could the Christian God of love and peace sanction such inhumanity under the guise of spreading the true faith?

After five hundred years of the glorification of bringing European Christian civilization to the indigenous peoples of the Americas, we are challenging this established rationale for destruction and are evaluating the utility of the Western European world view. The same cultural perspective which allowed the conquest and destruction of cultures in the New World now threatens to destroy the entire world. Five hundred years after your voyage we are rededicating ourselves to survival. Our survival as distinct cultures and the survival of the natural world which sustains all humanity are the two most important issues which we face today.

Although you would never know that you had made contact with another continent, other Europeans driven by greed will continue the cycles of conquest, slaughter, and destruction. These centuries of atrocities will all be sanctioned in the name of the true European Christian religion. It is ironic to note that partially as a result of your voyage, the self-certainty and unquestionable authority of the Catholic Church will begin to erode. As information from the New World spreads across Europe, the strict explanations of religious dogma will begin to lose credibility. Ultimately the authority of the church will be challenged as Catholic Europe divides into Protestant and Catholic countries which engage in savage religious wars all in the name of God. Not even fellow Christians in Western Europe will find compassion or escape from the destructive force of the Western world view. As Catholic Europe breaks apart, each country will struggle for a piece of the New World in order to enrich themselves and again rationalize everything as spreading another true religion to the heathens. The Spanish, Portuguese, French, English, and Dutch will colonize the New World and engage in great wars to maintain their territories as they pillage great wealth from the Americas.

European greed combined with religious conviction will rationalize the conquest and enslavement of millions of Native Peoples for centuries. As Europeans took gold and silver during the first two centuries of contact, many other significant contributions of the native cultures were ignored. Within two hundred years the great wealth will be plundered and Spain will collapse as a world power. However, the simple crops and medicines used by the peoples of the Americas will have a greater impact on the peoples of the world than all the gold and silver taken to Europe. These contributions to humanity will go unrewarded for centuries but will result in improved nutrition and health for the world.

As Spain declined in power a new force arose in North America. The same pattern of conquest, destruction and colonization by self-assured Europeans will again take place. However the new power will be English Protestants. In the north Catholic colonization will be surpassed by Anglo-Saxon Protestants. The new Protestant conquistadores will sweep across America, knowing that only their religion and their culture is true and valuable. The native peoples will again be conquered, enslaved and converted by the superior Christian movement. The Protestant Americans will know that God has chosen them to conquer the entire continent and then to conquer nature. About four hundred years after your voyage the colonization of the New World is complete and European countries turned to Africa and Asia for further conquest.

The world has been transformed by this unending cycle of greed and conquest. Ultimately Euro-american cultures expanded and developed world capitalism which allowed them to exploit the entire world. The changes that brought a breakdown in the authority of the church will eventually give rise to a Western view of nature called "science". Together science and capitalism will accelerate the process of development or bringing the benefits of European civilization to the world.

Within the last one hundred years more technological changes have occurred than within the last two thousand years. Although there have been great scientific and technological breakthroughs, the motivation of greed and conquest of peoples and nature continues to drive Euro-american culture. At the beginning of this century most people thought that science would replace religion as the salvation of humanity and would bring a new age of plenty.

Now at the end of this century the whole Western European world view is being seriously questioned. During the past fifty years, human greed has been transformed by science and global capitalism into an unending cycle of global destruction. Technology has brought about improvements and has created new problems. Now it appears that technology is no longer the savior but the destroyer. As science and global capitalism expanded to make profits under the guise of bringing superior European civilization to the world, countless poisons were created and released. We are now at the crossroads in which the very existence of mankind is threatened by Euro-american civilization.

Greed and technology have destroyed the great tropical forests of the world and poisoned the oceans. The air is not safe to breathe and the water is not safe to drink. The invisible ozone layer which has protected the world from harmful rays of the sun is eroding. Scientific leaders are now discussing when the destruction of our world began. For us we know the cycle of destruction began five hundred years ago. Just as the native peoples of the New World were threatened by your arrival five hundred years ago, now all the peoples of the world are threatened by the Western European world view which sees man as above nature.

Five hundred years after your voyage the old idea of superior Western European "scientific" civilization is no longer valid. We peoples of the New World look to our past for the answers which European culture cannot provide. The wisdom of our ancestors which was dismissed as insignificant superstitions by Europeans is now the only hope for the survival of the world. Our ancestors lived in harmony with the natural world and saw themselves as part of nature. Now this understanding is the only valid world view for the future generations of the world. The very peoples who were seen as savage heathens had perfected a greater knowledge which the European cultures lacked. This is, mankind is part of the natural world. Respect for the Earth brings prosperity; disregard for the Earth invites disaster. As we observe the five hundredth anniversary of your voyage, we also observe the decline of the Western European world view. We now dedicate ourselves and the future generations to the view of our ancestors. Human beings are the caretakers of the world and must work to maintain harmony with nature for the future generations. This sacred duty is more important than all the wealth or power an individual can try to accumulate in their lifetime.

Sincerely,

Charles C. Muzny
(Cherokee)

Dear Christopher:

As a direct and indirect result of your "voyage" to our islands, we, indigenous people of the Americas, are collectively recovering from 500 years of genocide. You see, you were not just a courageous adventurer. If one reads *The Journal of Christopher Columbus*, translated by Cecil Jane, it's clear that you paved the way for mass destruction of indigenous peoples, our cultures, between 1492 and 1992. Simply, we are the truth and survived to tell it.

Indian time. First, the Hopis of Arizona remind us that it has been only *twenty minutes* since your arrival. We have been here for millions and millions of years. And the idea that we have been here for a mere 28,999 years, according to the last dig, has really confused the issue. You see, it's not a "New World," as you would have us believe.

The "ice bridge" theory. Moreover, another misconception should be cleared. The Bering strait theory is wrong in one respect; *we went to Asia from here*, and not the other way around. This "data" comes from our oral tradition. We did not come from Asia, as the written European texts suggest. European scholars have tried for years to convince us that they differ widely on when we first arrived, and have some consensus on how we came, over the "ice bridge."

Indigenous oral tradition. Our elders say we went to Asia because our creation stories, our origin stories, root us to this land. It's the written history that attempts to confuse the issue. Why? White scholars want to think of the Americas, including North America, as a place filled with people from other countries. In their way of thinking, even the Indians came from some other place. If the American Indian people came from Asia, their logic goes, then this place was an empty desert, to use a metaphor, waiting for people to come here and make a garden of it, another metaphor. Of course this isn't true.

For 500 years, 1492-1992, Europeans have tried to justify the conquest, by rationalizing that we are all outsiders, as if the newcomers have the natural right to displace us. Now we understand the "ice theory," an idea that sustains the colonization of indigenous peoples, and of plants, rocks, trees, including land.

Furthermore, everything had a name. In renaming our islands and trees, our plants and rivers, our oceans and lakes, even our nations, you attempted to confuse us. Our surreal experience, then, began with the renaming.

All of this is a preface for understanding genocide.

You see, when the actor Marlon Brando was interviewed by a major tv newscaster, she asked, "Why haven't you made *the* film?" He replied, "For ten years, I have tried to make *the* film, a film of the American genocide of American Indians." He paused. "Hollywood won't make it." Why?

It's still difficult for Americans to see their real history. So they tend to distort history.

We are recovering from genocide. And it all started with your 1492 voyage to our country.

In *The Journal of Christopher Columbus,* you say we did not have a religion. You could not see it because the people did not pray as you did. So you tried to convince the world that we were without spirituality or souls. Your mission, then, was to civilize us, to make us into workers for Spain. We became your red gold.

And yet, in your book you say, "...I do not know the language, and the people of these islands do not understand me, nor I or anyone I have with me understand them. These Indians also, whom I carry with me, I often misunderstand...because many times they have attempted to escape."

You kidnapped us and wondered why we wanted to escape? You say you couldn't understand us and still projected untrues! You knew what you were doing. You wanted gold and silver and land. You terrorized us with steel and death and expected us to think you were gods.

The Spanish that followed you came with the same ideas. They soon discovered our achievements, though. According to *Native Mesoamerican Spirituality* by Miguel Leon-Portilla, our ancestors had precise systems of measuring the passing of time and had various forms of writing and were in possession of such things as a calendar. This we know, even though the Spanish burned our books, because "The post-Conquest recording of the texts lasted a period of some 70 years (1530-1600) and the material comprised poetry, mythology, song, oratory, fragments of plays, temple hymns, sages, and folklore." Between 1890 and 1910 some individuals were again working to revive the ancient texts.

We have survived. How? I agree with Leon-Portilla when he says, "The pre-Columbian spirit and oral legacy undoubtedly aided the Indian to survive into our times. And he has survived, against the most crushing, overwhelming odds. Through the centuries the Ancient Word and the lyric songs have given heart and courage to the individual as they did 500 years ago."

A lot of our texts, "books," did escape destruction.

In North America, to get closer to home, we have had our genocidal experiences documented. Ishi symbolizes this. The demographic effects of your "discovery" are documented in *American Indian Holocaust and Survival* by Russell Thornton. And the results of the technology that followed has failed. Those results are best seen in *In the Absence of the Sacred: The Failure of Technology and the Survival of the Indian Nations* by Jerry Mander. You see, we have documented proof of your negative impact on our lives and peoples.

As an indigenous poet said, recently, our last free year was 1491. Sine that time we have survived and resisted the genocide and collective confusion. We did this with spirituality, our way of seeing the world. Our philosophy has to do with the circle of life. You see, we knew the world was round and not flat. Ours is not a linear thinking philosophy. We see the circle as our symbol. We think in symbols and we think holistically. Everything in the circle is sacred. Nothing is outside the circle, not the rocks, trees, water, or two-legged beings.

For us the world is not new. We kept the pipe, sweat lodge, and peyote ceremonies. We are "indians" because we honor Indians. We honor the old people, and we honor the earth. And we acknowledge the four sacred colors: red, white, yellow, and black. Symbols for the four races of the world.

Those individuals who grew away from our traditions are making a full circle and returning to them. That's documented in *Night Flying Woman*, a Minnesota Historical Society publication. We kept our oral traditions for our seventh generations.

Finally, to honor our people we are organizing and participating in a spiritual run that begins this April, 1992, and finishes October 12, 1992. We will run from South America and from North America and we will meet in Teotihuacan, the metropolis which was at its zenith around the fifth century A.D., and is now called Mexico

City. You see, we survived 500 years of genocide, that's our message.

Sincerely,

Dave Gonzales
(Yaqui)

Dear Christopher:

listening
centuries beneath this Southern sand
I hear the dark hurt of hunted souls
reaching to the great white bloom of sail,
new sound of chain over gunwale,
light-skinned voices
cutting with tongues of gold
sharper than any stone,
and the will to put fire to dwelling,
fire to temple;
the will; always the will,
     fe y oro

listening
for my ancestor's voice,
I see her raptor face
her black hair;
I hear her keening,
nights on bloody paths,
burnt scrub oak and pine,
broken villages,
running wounds,
far from any shaman's heaven.

I see her flint eyes;
I have turned them up
with my racial memory's plow,
arrowheads of deep hatred
where rains have drowned
the dance
and the corn is gone to rot,
and the fires no longer shakes
their weapons in the night.

for her, and every morning,

Dear Christopher

my heart raises new stone blades
against new Spanish sails --
hotels, restaurants,
condos on the beach.

old Creek women
take the earth's own shape,
but this has not made them quiet.
their eyes have become my arrows;
their distant voices
power the thunder in my words.

Sincerely,

Paul Rice
(Creek)

Dear Christopher:

I am not one who usually writes letters, especially letters on emotionally loaded topics, however I felt compelled to write this one. The nation-wide celebration in your honor has sparked heightened awareness of Native American rights, issues, and causes: lengthy topics in their own right. This letter however, although addressed to you, Mr. Columbus, deals with two issues from an individual perspective that will hopefully have significance to all Native peoples. The issues are of conflict: conflict between two worlds, Native American concerns and scientific explorations of Native America's past, especially regarding the reburial issue. The other conflict lies within myself caught between both of these worlds. Yes, I am a cultural-less ethnic renegade, whose actual blood line is Navajo. My conflict is not purely ethnic, but within a new chasm--I am also an archaeologist. Therefore the purpose of this letter is two-fold: one, define the conflicting issues as I perceive them, and two, present my solution.

Of the two major conflicts, I will deal with the latter first. To explain a little of who I am and the nature of my cultural baggage. When asked, "what is your ethnic background?" as many people, for unknown reasons, inevitably do, I usually bumble around, "Chicano...," "Mexican American...," "...although my family is actually Navajo, you know...," until I finally settle with "I'm an anthropologist." This usually elicits chortles amongst anthropologists, sociologists, or psychologists, but most others merely look bewildered, shrug, and finish asking whatever they intended, before I rambled on what they thought would be a short answer. Why am I not certain of my ethnic affiliation? Well I am now--I am an anthropologist. Some would ask, "is an ethnic identity important at all?" It is important, especially for those who perceive themselves in a pseudo-cultural vacuum. You see, Mr. Columbus, you have helped create a long list of people, I suspect, who feel lost between cultures; they [have] a longing to feel connected to Indian people and culture, yet not feeling right about it somehow. Mr. Columbus, the periods of colonialism, in the 15th, 16th, 17th and 18th centuries in the Americas, were ruled by annihilation of native peoples--pure genocide, (bet you didn't think it would take over 500 years). The 19th and early 20th centuries were more covert; government policies attempted to assimilate Native peoples. This was cultural genocide.

I am the latest end product of a "cultural assimilation program." The U.S. government enacted policies to deal with Indian people, to turn them into Euro-American white folk. Therefore they began to relocate many different Indian people to California from the four corners area in the mid-1940s. The most suitable for the relocation, the government found, were the young adults of this period. They consisted mostly of first generations of Indians to grow up with little influence from their grandparents who could remember traditional ways. My maternal grandmother was one of these to be transplanted from southern Colorado to southern California. My maternal great-grandmother was dispirited to see her go, but truly believed that life would be easier for both. This was the most tragic part of the program; not only had the government convinced themselves what they were doing was best for the Indians, but they had convinced the Indians. My grandmother quickly married and had my mother soon after arriving in California. It was a desperate time, first my grandmother was removed from her homeland and then my mother [was] attempting to understand her new homeland. The need to belong motivated them to deny their true origins. I was, therefore, the third generation brought up as a "non-Indian/Indian, whatever [that is]. "It was for my own good."

This search for ethnic acceptance and identity, as with many anthropologists, I suspect, has guided me into the career choices that I have made. I understand where my family came from and the cultures they cast aside to be accepted. Yet, the more I understand from others' experiences, the more I realize that they taught me more of what I initially thought was lost. My traditional culture is buried within me. I needed to know more. I wasn't satisfied with reading ethnographic accounts of salvage anthropologists that were interpreted through Euro-American eyes. I needed to see the past, and be able to interpret it myself--I became an archaeologist. My job is to unravel the "truth" that lies under our feet. If there is such a thing as "truth" about the past of native peoples, I believe it will only be through looking directly into its small remnants that it can be understood.

The Native American/science conflict is a very complicated and sensitive issue, one that is still ambivalent in my heart. It is a topic that has thrust me into several heated emotional debates and I have felt alienated on too many occasions. The most unfortunate aspect of this entire debate seems to rest [on] a single subject, that in actuality is a minor part of most excavations. I will attempt to present the sides of the debate via a true life example.

I worked on a project as an experienced member of a crew on a typical site in southern California. There were tribal representatives on site acting as monitors. I normally worked in the lab on this project; however the excavation was now concentrating on a particularly sensitive area and the monitors requested my presence. The request initially stroked my ego, because I felt that monitors trusted me, both as an experienced archaeologist and as a distant kin, perhaps. I have always been firm in my belief in honesty and the necessity for no bull shit. I must admit, the majority of the crew was very nervous around Native American monitors and some outright resented their presence. I however, have always felt comfortable and learned from their presence: learned not so much historic or ethno-archaeological information, but more personal friendly insights like, whose cousin is actually so-and-so's uncle, and whose brother-in-law is actually whose third cousin. These were stories of real people, living real lives, with genuine concerns and strong convictions.

Friday afternoon (these things always happen on Fridays) we hit the bone material and I was faced with the pressure of answering the question no one wanted to hear, "were they human?" They were in very poor condition (this was an early site), and they lay under a calcim-carbonate layer of dissolving fossil shellfish, but they were most certainly human. I had never felt so alone in my entire life. The archaeologist inside was unbelievably excited; these were the only non-cremated remains found in this entire region; the data that could be ascertained from this burial was one-of-a-kind. Yet, these were quite possibly the remains of one of the monitor's great great...grand parents and the looks on their faces were of sorrow. Fear of a weekend disturbance, they recommended I remove the material, place them in a non-synthetic bag (in this case leather) and temporarily store them until Monday, so they could consult with elders. They could not understand my desire to touch the bones and although I could appreciate and respect their feeling of polluting of their spirits, I could not completely understand them either. They were stored until Monday.

I was the first to arrive Monday morning to a mob of reporters, Indian activists and those I believed my friends with angry scowls on their faces. The activists, in feathers and beads were demanding the return of the remains to the ground and the project termination. The tribal representatives were asking to be heard and have their ancestor's remains cared for and respected. The site monitors were now accusing me of playing the white-mans game and acting as a puppet. The reporters just stood around trying to record anyone who could be most vocal and look good for TV. The principle investigator arrived and held a very nervous news conference. To this day I don't understand why, but he outright lied about the remains that everyone knew were in the next room. It was at that moment I realized the issue had nothing to do with remains, but legitimization of Indian people. Although I was in the middle of two worlds, they were struggling to define their one. They are fighting one of the few things that could actually help solve the problem--archaeology. This is the persecutive that has come to an equilibrium in my heart.

You see, Mr. Columbus, your ancestors have now convinced our ancestors to fight over crumbs and emotional issues and not live together as people. A friend refers to this as the "delegitimization of Indian people", and another calls it the "I'm more Indian than thou syndrome." There must be a solution.

I believe that it is *my* ancestors, albeit distant, that have many stories waiting to be understood. The real, untainted past, the "truth," if you will, of real people who actually did discover this continent, is still waiting to be found. This is my plea to native peoples. Why are there so few Native American archaeologists? There are many serving as tribal representatives for monitoring sites at excavations, but no MA or Ph.D level principle investigator managing their own projects. It is native peoples who should most benefit from the rediscovery of past societies. In fact in the southwest, archaeology has been essential to settling land disputes between the Hopi and the Navajo. Land was returned to Taos Pueblo because archaeology "proved" their ancestors lived around Blue Lake. Yet, I am alienated again by many native people for taking this perspective. When I argue for more native peoples in archaeology, I mean all aspects, including, dare I say, burials.

Yes, I have and will work on Native burials. Why? Because if I don't take the responsibility myself to understand how to identify, excavate, analyze, and learn from remains that are going to be removed, I will be slave to someone else's interpretation of my relatives. I do not have a religious conflict with remains and many Native people do, but there is no conflict with plastic casts to learn from. I worked too many sites as a grade monitor where bone was exposed; my ignorance frustrated me, until I could contact someone else, inevitably a non-Indian, to identify the material. Now I am in control without having to wait. It is a very sensitive issue, one that might be best handled by people who claim to be their ancestors. I have worked with Cahuilla, Pachanga, Gabrielino, Kuwiasu, Navajo, Chumash, and others on several sites, some with burials and have received positive feedback from most of them. Most have at one time or another encouraged me to enroll and just monitor and stop digging. And I always encourage them to go back to school and start their own firm. It is, after all, the Native peoples that have the most to learn from archaeology and the most to lose if it's stopped.

This letter is written from the heart, by someone who only wishes to learn, rediscover, and understand his ancestor's prehistory. It would be a terrible blow to science if it were all stopped. If the card-carrying activists would reevaluate their causes and if people could work as one, the real goals could be achieved. Someone once argued that there aren't enough anthropologists to analyze the remains we have in storage now. I would argue yes, we do; they are waiting for the depoliticalization of the issue. Everyone argues that not enough archaeological reports are written for people to read and learn from. I say why don't we take it upon ourselves to excavate, write, learn, and teach our own history: because, Columbus, that is nearly all we have left.

Sincerely,

John Torres
(Navajo)

Dear Christopher:

I am sending you greetings on the eve of the 500th anniversary of your momentous discovery of the New World. Lest you be concerned, I assure you that you are still a very popular figure here and your anniversary certainly will not be forgotten. In fact, plans are already underway for a world-wide celebration in your honor. Dignitaries and officials will all be out in hordes to tell us once again about the immense consequences of your great voyage. There will even be three special replicas of your little ships which will retrace your journey from Spain to the West Indies. That should please you.

It will also be a time for a renewal of the many quarrels and arguments that have developed over the circumstances of your voyage, that parade of enigmas and unanswered questions about which you left us to wonder. This may surprise you, Chris, but not everyone is satisfied with the pat story that has come down to us in the history books. In fact, one of the more amazing things that has developed since you left us is the disagreement over the kind of person you were and what you were really trying to do.

The most widely held belief is that your success in discovering America was mostly luck, that you had only the vaguest idea of where you were going and that finding a new land was sheer accident, as fortunate as striking the lottery. And worst, you never realized what you had actually found.

This is a simple, harmless story. But others are not so kind, for you have also been portrayed as an ignorant, illiterate, self-seeking fortune hunter who did not hesitate to use deceit and exaggerations to reach your ends. Your success in finding the Indies depended more on willful stubbornness and vanity than on knowledge or skill. These two contrary beliefs somehow satisfy those who would demean your great achievement and at the same time please those who like to make heroes out of unlikely cloth. And of course, there may be some truth in each, enough to raise a continuing controversy. Only you know, Chris, only you.

What is so amazing is that there is still so much doubt and uncertainty about your life and your discovery. Not just about a few aspects, Chris, but about everything. Crews of scholastic scavengers have been hard at work in the trash bins of history seeking any scrap that will clarify the endless questions they conjure up. And these questions are legion. You would squirm in your grave if you could read some of the fables that have been concocted about you. Or perhaps you would just laugh.

On the other hand, you should not become too distressed, for rest assured that for most people there is no Columbus problem. You long ago became a folk hero, a mythological person straight from a grade school history book. You discovered America in 1492, and that is that! And with each year that passes, you become more and more heroic, a courageous figure forever staunch at the helm, sailing across the ocean blue. Nations clamor to claim you as their own. The Spanish, the Italians, the Portuguese all bicker and quarrel over your birthplace. It has become a matter of great national pride. You left this issue confused, Chris, and even your son Ferdinand seems a little uncertain about your origins. Why the mystery, Chris? Did you really think it was necessary to hide your ancestry, however humble, from the eyes of history? That is not the American way, not the American way at all.

But this is only one small issue. For others there are far more intriguing puzzles. I'm sure you realize that many of these questions have little merit and only reflect the fact that clever, imaginative minds can always find ways of questioning great historical events, especially ones that took place so long ago and left so little factual record. But nevertheless they still haunt us, and will no doubt fuel the debates that will rage as your anniversary approaches.

You would be astonished at the disagreements that have revolved around the simple question of your education and character. Damn it, Chris, did you or did you not go to school and learn how to read, write, and cipher? Are you aware that of all the letters and notes you wrote, the only ones we still possess are in Spanish, and not very good Spanish either, I'm told. A few phrases in Latin, but no Portuguese or Italian. That seems strange if indeed you were Italian or a long time resident of Portugal. It gives you an idea of why questions are still being raised though.

But if you didn't go to school, how did you acquire your knowledge of geography and navigation? Did you learn these skills in your youth as you journeyed from one end of the Mediterranean to the other like some peripatetic medieval jet-setter? Were you sailor, tourist or merchant man? You left us dangling, Chris. Then there was that little military excursion to North Africa for the royal house of Anjou. Was that a tall story, Chris?

The question still remains that if you were as ignorant and uncouth as some contend, how did you accomplish so much? You must have possessed some worthwhile qualities to have become the captain of a vessel when twenty-six years old, as has been claimed, and a master mariner when twenty-seven. Surely these are extraordinary achievements for a supposedly uneducated, illiterate young Italian handicapped by living in a foreign land. How was it that you, a poor ignorant peasant of a sailor, nevertheless managed to marry a woman from a well-known upper-class family in Lisbon, gain an audience with the King of Portugal to discuss your wild ideas, and after being rejected there, gain additional audiences with the King and Queen of Spain? I suspect here is much more than luck involved here, Chris.

Despite all this, there remain many doubts about your sailing and navigational skills, or how you acquired such capabilities as you had. However, I don't find that as mysterious as others, for it seems obvious to me that the many years of work in your brother Bartholomeo's map shop in Lisbon would have provided ample exposure to every map, chart and idea then available. I doubt you could have drawn the exact and detailed navigational charts required by mariners without either great personal experience or good prior charts to work from.

That there were maps aplenty is well known. Of course, we would like to be certain just which maps you studied and how much they influenced you. Unfortunately, you never say. I'm sure Ptolemy's world map of 150 A.D., for example, was a standard reference available to you. But did you have an opportunity to study the map Marco Polo brought back from China and which Fra Mauro apparently used as a basis for his 1459 map of the Orient? How did it compate with Marino Stanudo's round map of the world of 1320? Or Grazioso Benincasa's 1479 chart which stretched out far enough into the Atlantic to show the Azores, Maderia and the fabled island of Antilla? The latter, I'm afraid, is only a stylized drawing presumably not meant to be an accurate representation, but merely to indicate the presence of land somewhere out beyond the Azores.

It seems more certain that you had an opportunity to study Tocanelli's chart of the world sent to Fernao Martin at Lisboa in 1474, which depicted the island of Zipangu (Japan) off the coast of China. Surely you saw Matellus's world map of 1489 which clearly locates Iceland, and beyond a Greenland still attached across the Arctic to Norway

But it is thought that of all these, the one that influenced you the most was Behaim's world map of 1490. Since Behaim was in Lisboa when you were there, did you have an opportunity to discuss this map with him? Did you ask him why he had drawn Zipangu bisected by the Tropic of Cancer when Polo, whom he apparently used as a source, was well aware that Japan was located in a cold temperate zone? Did not these various ideas about the shape of the earth stimulate and influence you own world concept? It seems impossible that you as a professional mapmaker would not have heard of or seen these numerous attempts to picture the world, or been aware of the problems they presented. After all, Prince Henry's famous school of navigational art was right there close at hand with its vast collection and its renowned scholars exchanging ideas daily. And what about the considerable collection of your father-in-law, Bartholomeo Perestrella, which his widow made available to you? If only we knew what it contained. The one map that is still attributed to you is an admirable piece of work, neat, concise, accurate, showing quite clearly that you were a skilled master craftsman of your trade. But we need a few more examples, then we would be certain. A simple word here and there, Chris, would have cleared up a lot of questions about your knowledge and ability.

You even confuse us with the vague comments about your trip to Iceland in 1477. You say you not only went to Iceland, presumably the port at Reykjevik, but three hundred miles beyond to latitude 73 degrees north. Of course, ten degrees is more than three hundred miles, but I gather you meant three hundred miles from the northern tip of Iceland. But that would have been brought you to the coast of Greenland at Cape Brewster or even Cape Perry, where the great glacier mountains are visible at sea. What were you after, and what did you see on this trip? And another thing; you casually mention that

Iceland was about the size of England. How did you know this, Chris? You fail to tell us!

Nor do you comment on the old Norse tales about Leif Ericson, and Vinland far to the west, told by every Icelander. Didn't these stories arouse your curiosity about what lay out there even if you couldn't always understand exactly what they were saying? You were far too perceptive and curious to have missed those clues, Chris, far too perceptive.

And then you left us a nice tidbit with the little story about the strange Oriental-appearing man and woman washed ashore at Galway, Ireland, whom you saw or heard about on your way back from Iceland. Did you really believe they were castaways from Lapland or Asia? Wasn't it obvious to you with your wide knowledge of Atlantic currents and tides that it was impossible to drift from Arctic Norway to the west coast of Ireland? Didn't those Eskimos with their strange Mongoloid features and sealskin clothes raise some questions in your mind? Weren't you intrigued by the possibility there might be something more than ice and barrens out there to the west? Yet you remained silent.

You were not much more helpful about your journey to the Portuguese trading post of Al Mina far down the African coast in 1478. Or perhaps you made more than one trip, since you indicate in your diary on November 12th, 1492 that you had often sailed from Africa to Portugal with natives aboard. Yet you neglected to tell the number of times or for what purpose you made these trips. Nevertheless, it seems certain that you had more than a passing familiarity with tropical Africa, enough to give you a very good idea of the size and shape of the earth. By then you travels had covered an arc of the earth's surface from Turkey three thousand miles west to the Azores, and five thousand miles from the Equator to 73 degrees north. You knew the quadrant from Al Mina to the North Pole was one-fourth of the earth's circumference, and since you had traversed eighty percent of that distance, you were certainly in a good position to make an accurate estimate of the full distance around the earth.

Yet it has been proposed that you underestimated the size of the earth and were confused because you were unable to take precise readings of the latitudes from the deck of a pitching ship. Consequently, you didn't have an accurate grasp of world topography or how far it was westward to the Orient. I find that highly unlikely, since I'm sure you were sensible enough to take these readings from firm ground in Iceland, Greenland, Ireland, the Azores, Maderia, the Canaries, Portugal and Al Mina. Furthermore, you were not the only one taking such measurements, for you mention that the great royal navigator Jose Vizinho was on board when you visited Al Mina. No, I feel you had accurate enough data. That is not the problem that bothers everyone.

Actually, there are two problems. One is perceived as your secretiveness and deviousness in providing an accurate account of your goals and knowledge, and two, the absolute certainty and persistence with which you pursued this venture.

How was it that you, a simple merchant sailor, became so convinced that you would be the one to reach the Spice Islands of the Orient by sailing west instead of east? There were many professional explorers and sea captains with better credentials than you who would have seemed more likely to have promoted this enterprise. Yet they didn't. What was it that you knew that they didn't?

Of course, the idea itself was not new, and discussions of sailing westward across the Atlantic were fairly common. The Portuguese king indeed had issued a royal grant to John Vogoda in 1462 to locate two islands lying west of the Azores. This action may have resulted from the expeditions of Diego de Tieves and Pedro de Velascos in 1452, which sailed 450 miles southwest of the Azores to the region of the Sargasso Sea. Other stories about strange sightings abounded. But you were a hard-headed, sensible man not easily persuaded by such reports. Ferdinand, your son, tells us you merely laughed about the silly tales of Antilla, or of St. Brendan, the wild Irishman who claimed to have found land to the west, or the other fanciful yarns about islands across the great ocean-sea. Yet, at the same time, he tells us you had been thinking about this project for many years and had read all the classical scholars and conducted many studies on your travels with this great adventure already in mind. And you must have detected something you thought would guarantee success, for why else would King John give a secret mandate to Fernao Dulmo to take two caravels in search of a great island, or a coast of a mainland, in the western Atlantic in 1486 immediately after refusing you such a grant? Just what did you say to him to convince him to undertake the expense of this expedition?

Furthermore, it would appear that you were quite familiar with these earlier grants, for your proposal to both King John of Portugal and the Spanish crown seems to have been closely modeled after those original version with all the standard demands for governorships, honors and titles.

The question of secretiveness and deviousness remains. There seems to be a great deal of confusion about this issue, especially about your destination. Some critics take literally everything you say, and others don't believe a word of it. Many don't realize there were good reasons for you to deliberately confuse your intentions. They are not aware that it was common practice at that time for merchants and sea captains not to reveal their routes, destinations, and other pertinent information. False charts, journals and records were often employed to mislead others so that a monopoly could be maintained over any discoveries. Some have thought you were deceitful but of course it was only self-protection. No one could be trusted, the sailors, the merchants, the royal houses, all could steal your information and use it to deprive you of your legitimate rights, which, in fact, is exactly what eventually happened to you. There was only one safe place for the crucial knowledge and that was in your head. I accept that you had to steer a careful course cleverly designed to convince while not revealing too much.

It seems to me there has also been a failure to recognize another reason for your vague or conflicting statements. You were totally dependent upon the largesse of others for the financing and support needed to outfit the expedition. I can see that in order to get the required backing it was necessary for you to appeal to their special interest, and this meant to a variety of people and groups each with its own expectations. Consequently you spun a different story to each: converting pagans for the church, finding gold and treasure for the merchants, and land and power for the monarchy. I realize, of course, that none of these necessarily represented your own primary interest.

So it is easy enough to understand why you were reluctant to set anything down or reveal your route or purpose too precisely. But it does make it hard for us today to reconstruct fully what you had in mind, and it certainly is one of the reasons there remain so many disagreements about you. Yet there can be no disagreements about the fact that you eventually overcame all obstacles and successfully completed the trip. Nevertheless, many people still question why you chose the route you did, and I also have pondered that question.

Of the three possible courses across the Atlantic, the northern, the central, and the southern, you chose the one that seems least promising. You had been to Iceland previously and it would have been relatively simple for you to retrace your steps to Greenland, which you presumably had sighted, and on to North America. The old Norse tales provided good evidence of land beyond Greenland. Furthermore, you were aware that shortly before your voyage, a ship commissioned by the Danish king and commanded by a Portuguese had reportedly visited both Greenland and Labrador. Yet you rejected that route. Was it because the Danes had found nothing but cold and snow or was it because you had no official sanction from Denmark for such a voyage and seemed unlikely to secure royal approval?

On the other hand, you could have used the central route through the Azores, islands which you also had visited earlier. This would have given you a launching station one thousand miles closer to your destination and almost halfway to Newfoundland. This, it seems to me, would have been the best choice. It has been said you did not use this route because of adverse currents and winds around the Azores. But that seems a spurious reason, for the Portuguese had little trouble reaching these islands on a regular basis. I suspect the middle route was actually your original choice, and you only abandoned it after the rejection of your proposal by King John in 1484 and the subsequent secret expedition he sent out to test your theory. When you transferred your allegiance to Spain, it became impossible to use the Azores under the semi-hostile relations which existed between the two countries.

So the southern route became the only feasible course left to you. Despite changing the direction of your course, however, you apparently didn't change your destination. Yet that created another set of problems, for how could you expect to reach Japan by steering a course so far south of the latitude of that nation? Surely you were aware from your intensive reading of Polo that Japan could not be reached by the route you took? Since there was a difference of at least ten degrees and eight hundred miles, was the error yours or Polo's?

Dear Christopher

In addition, Polo's journal locates Japan 1500 miles east of China. Weren't you suspicious of this figure? Just prior to Polo's arrival in 1261, the Great Khan had launched an ill-prepared attack on that island kingdom, and several years later a second invasion was staged with equally disastrous results. Since Polo was present during the second attack, he must have known Japan was not 1500 miles from the mainland, as no sensible general would attempt an invasion of that mighty nation across such a span of open sea.

Even more important, the Chinese had the most advanced maps and mapping techniques in the world at that time. Phei Hsui's manual of instructions for constructing accurate grided maps was written in 267 A.D. and was widely used. A magnificent scale-accurate, grided map of China made in 1134 A.D. exists today in a stone copy and was well known during Polo's time and was undoubtedly seen by him. Maps of China and the adjacent regions were common and extensively used in the bureaucratic and military affairs of the government. As a bureaucrat under the Khan's administration, Polo must have been aware of them. Furthermore, in his own travels through eastern China and later to the South China Sea, Java, Sumatra and Malaysia, he indicated he had a good understanding of the location of the various important islands and their relationships to one another. Yet he never mentions Zipangu which, according to Toscanelli's map, he could scarcely avoid. How then was he so far off with respect to the location of Japan, which as a matter of fact can on occasion be seen from the Asiatic mainland? Is it possible there was a translation error here, or as is more likely, did the European mapmakers confuse Japan with Taiwan? The representation of Zipangu on Tascanelli's map not only has the shape of Taiwan, but accurately shows the Tropic of Cancer bisecting the island.

Another thing that puzzles me, Chris, is that if your destination was actually the Indies and Japan, why is it that the lengthy contract with King Ferdinand says nothing about those countries? It merely states you were "authorized to discover and acquire certain islands and mainlands in the Ocean sea." It even repeats this later: "Some of the said islands and mainland will be acquired by your pains and industry." This doesn't sound like there was much intent to try to reach the Orient.

But even more ludicrous is the idea that you with three small ships and ninety men without a single soldier among them intended to arrive in China or Japan and lay claim to all those lands and riches in the name of the distant King and Queen of Spain, and proclaim yourself governor. Surely you jest, Chris, for of all people you were aware from Polo of the size and might of the Chinese armies, the most powerful military forces in the world. How then did you seriously expect to lay claim to these vast lands and gain access to their riches mentioned in the proposal to the King and Queen in the face of such realities? This is arrogance, Chris.

What was your purpose, then, for you must have had something in mind?

Some people would ask us to believe you would set out on a voyage such as yours without knowing where you were going, how far it was, or how long it would take. And that you would risk your life as well as the lives of ninety men, and three ships on an expedition into the unknown ocean without having gathered all the information you could or without considering all the possibilities. This doesn't seem reasonable, even for a man as bold and confident as you. Therre must have been more to it than that.

After all, you had many years experience as a ship's officer and were fully aware of the many constraints that governed the scope of any long sea voyage. This included the distance your caravels could sail in a day, the amount of supplies the crews required, and the time the craft could remain in the water before the hulls needed cleaning and repair. Therefore, you were quite able to calculate the approximate distance that marked the limits of your projected voyage before you ever set foot on the deck of the Santa Maria. You also knew the crew, the officers and the king's advisors could estimate these factors as readily as you. It was unlikely that your ships could average more than eighty miles a day in both good and bad weather. The crew could be expected to use a minimum of 100 gallons of liquid a day, or 750 pounds, and 100 pounds of food plus wood-fuel and other necessities. A thirty-day voyage, therefore, would cover about 2400 miles and use 3000 gallons of liquid, or 12 tons, and several tons of food and fuel. But since you had to plan on another thirty days for the return in the event you found nothing, it was necessary to carry double the above amounts. Even your public estimations of the distance to the Orient, which you deliberately shortened to make your project seem more feasible, would have required several times those amounts.

With these things in mind then, Chris, did you really expect to sail as far as the Indies or Japan, more than 215 degrees of longitude or 60 percent of the distance around the world, with the supplies you could carry aboard That is 15000 miles at the equator and 13500 at the latitude of your course. Even if you truly underestimated the size of the earth by half, that still left 6700 miles between Spain and your destination. I realize you didn't know the longitude of Japan, or how far the coast of China or the Indies extended eastwards, but Polo and the maps you had gave you a reasonable estimate. And it is true you reduced the distance by resupplying at the Canaries, but nevertheless, your own experience would have told you that it would be difficult if not impossible to reach the Far East with the supplies your ships could carry. And if you knew this before you left Spain, just how did you intend to resolve this problem?

The only conclusion is that you either intended to turn back at the point where half your supplies were exhausted or you had strong reason to expect to be able to replenish them somewhere. Your journal implies you knew you were at the point of forced return when land was finally sighted. That might explain your increasing anxiety, but what explains your assurance?

Well, Chris, it is time to close now, but this will give you an idea of the kinds of questions that still remain unanswered after all these centuries. They continue to puzzle and intrigue, forcing us to examine the paltry evidence over and over again, trying to squeeze out any new insights or clarifications about your motives and intentions.

But all this could have been avoided, Chris, if only you had looked ahead and realized the problems your scanty notes, your failure to be precise, your inconsistencies, would create. These omissions and failures are so pervasive and critical one begins to wonder if they were not deliberate. Is that it, Chris? Was all this obfuscation deliberately planned so that in the advent your voyage did not gain you the immortality you sought, the enigmas and questions you left behind surely would? If that was your plan, Chris, you succeeded well.

Sincerely,

Charles C. Case
(Nacirema)

Dear Christopher:

Accept this as a view of a 20th century native person from the shore of this western hemisphere to Christopher, Cortes, Castile, and the Mayflower.

The news spread quickly across the land. It was whispered in the mountains and in the vast valleys that there might be a fulfilling of the legend of Quetzacoatl-- that he returned from the morning star as it is said that he promised with passion as he was thrust out of his homeland, a land which lies to the south and upon the sunrise side of the world.

We were certain that the son-of-morning star had returned. We learned that he and his tribe entered the land with much anger and longed to destroy those that had put him out of his position as Cacique. The message came from the south and from the east--as the Mohawk and the Seminole knew of the legend for many seasons, and they, too, waited and wondered.

It is known that Quetzacoatl was thrust from his domain because he was an honored Cacique and worked the earth with his people. He brought new methods of growing corn and devised new plans for growing cotton of many colors so painting cloth was no longer necessary. With his dreams he designed manners of watering the earth and he helped the people make food and fruit grow where there once was only a harsh landscape.

Quetzacoatl taught the people to be good and to share the bounty of earth. He said that the bounty of earth belonged to all of the people all of the time and that the children should be served first at the feast, then the elders, then the people. He said that this is the manner of survival of the most valuable of our elements, the children. The children must eat first because of their youth, the elders second because of their wisdom and their ability to teach the children, and the people who were not yet wise but were distant from being a child, third-- because labor was their love and to feed the elders and the children their duty. Together they worked the earth and sang songs to the rising sun and to the vastness of the universe, and to all creatures dwelling upon earth and everywhere between the stars.

When the kings and those of great power and jealousy ran him out of the land with anger (for the people loved him truly), he vowed to return with thunder and lightning--to reclaim his just position among the people. The lessons say that if he returns on one-deer*, he will strike the children. If on one-jaguar*, he will strike all of the people whomsoever. But if he returns on one-reed*, he will strike *only* kings.

The Kings trembled.

That is how the story came to my people dwelling upon the western edge of our world near the thundering waters of the outer-ocean. Our creation is beside the crashing and murmuring waters of the rivers and under the canopy of dancing stars where the unknowable dwells forever.

We know that they came from the direction of the rising sun and the morning star. But we also know that they are not Quetzacoatl. We know that they did not return to claim a just seat among the people and the governing body. We know that they have not the power to love the earth and to sing songs in the early morning as the bright star looks across the silence and dawn is silver-green upon the horizon.

They landed in the south on the sunrise side of our earth and destroyed the pueblos. Their commander was invisible. Their commander gave them orders to destroy our people and to take possession of all of our earth. Their commander, God, made them claim all of the earth of our people for a king and a queen who dwelled somewhere to the east. Their God was angry with our people, commanding the strangers to slaughter us, it is said, in order to save us.

It would be many seasons before we would be able to understand them and to learn more about their God. Kings trembled. Kings and those honoring the fierce kings.

* * * *

It was not the passing of many seasons and we learned that there was another entry of strangers into our homeland. Again, we wondered. They entered upon the eastern shore of the great salt waters where the nation of the Narragansett roamed in vast numbers under the summer sun and danced with the beating of their infinite hearts in a vast circle, singing.

They, too, had a God to lead them and to command them. Their God, too, was angry and had no tolerance for my people. They, too, came with methods of destruction and they appeared to have no honor for earth and the goodness of earth within their being. Their God told them to be masters over us and their God also told them that we had no spirit that, therefore, it was not only reasonable to destroy us but destroying us would find glorification within His kingdom.

Their God gave them our land and none of our chiefs can remember the season when their God petitioned our councils asking if he could have the earth in order to give it away. But God took it and he gave it to strangers who walk upon earth in anger, feast in anger, dream in anger, move in anger, think in anger. We wondered long about this God. We suffered in our wondering. Across the land councils gathered, chiefs spoke. Trembling, they wondered of this God.

What was this two-footer who entered our land led by a strange God? What is this God who takes from our people and condemns us as if we had no right to dwell upon the earth and to sing songs of all of life as is our intended purpose? What is God doing here? Where did God come from? What tribe does he belong to? How long will God linger?

All of these questions were before the councils gathered at the fires in the evening. Many council fires burned through the night. The answer refused to appear. The answer, too, was invisible.

We learned to read the speaking leaf and here is what earth-children have discovered.

It is said that there have always been many invisible Gods of the people who dwell in the lands beyond the eastern salt waters. It is said that their Gods have always been jealous. In anger their Gods cast them to the winter winds. In anger their Gods force them from their homelands. In anger their Gods lead them to "promised lands."

In anger their Gods wrote laws upon stone for them to abide by. In anger their Gods demand obedience from them and threaten their children with everlasting hell-fire. In anger their Gods crushed other nations in order to "plant" His *chosen* people upon lands that are precious to original nations of the world. In anger their Gods intruded into the lives of many people and bid his "flock" to follow--seeking neither permission to enter or pardon for the intrusion.

In anger their God battled with Satan and with other Gods and made wars upon wars, put nation against nation, moved tribe against tribe and brother against sister. And, when the wars between the Gods finally settled, it was impossible to identify that which was truly of a Satanic nature and that which was truly Godly. The native people of this word have not yet been able to discern between them.

This is what the speaking leaf told us. Charlot of the Flatheads spoke to the council saying:

We were happy when he first came. We first thought he came from the light; but he comes like the dusk of evening now, not like the dawn of morning. He comes like a day that has passed, and night enters our future with him.

The speaking leaf taught us that the wanderings of God were always met with conflict and confrontation. Long ago, it is said, children were ejected from their homeland and were led by God through the wilderness. He parted bodies of water so the people might pass through walking upon the earth below the waters in their search for peace and happiness--and land.

God commanded the people without ever uttering a sound. And that which worried our council of elders most of all was that God stood far away from the people - dwelling and watching from that distant and invisible place, heaven. Their God was not within their being, not protecting their spirit, not encompassing their purpose-- but watching their movements to see if they dared to place another god above Him. He watched, always alert, always prepared to strike the "flock."

They said that they "heard" his voice. But my people gathered at the sacred fire and listened to all of the sounds of the universe, yet heard no command from the invisible God. A God that lived beyond the spirit and beyond the being of the people who feared him.

Yes, they feared their God!

Their God thundered to them that He would condemn them for all seasons if they failed to obey his wishes. Their God told them that my native people were not real, that we were cannibals and savages, that we were less than animals; that we dwelled in a land that we knew not how to manage, and that we had no connection between our spirit and the power that turns the earth around the sun and the sun around a greater wonder. By his "word,' their invisible God condemned my people to death.

*   *   *   *

After being cast from their homeland those thinking themselves "pure," gathered at Scrooby--which is a dwelling place in the eastern lands. Soon they were cast from Scrooby and, after wandering for years, the God-people cast their covetous eyes to the shores of my people, the earth of our dreams, the world of our vision. Their God, as had the God of "the children," could penetrate our domain. He failed to seek permission to enter. He, instead, trespassed into the world of the native nations and issued to His children a right to occupy.

They came with their "Book-Of-One-Great-Law" in one hand-- and guns in the other.

From the floating long-house called *The Flower of Spring*, it is said, they entered the lands of the Narragansett, the Wampanoag, the Mashpee near the dancing waters called Nantucket. There the native nations fed them. There, also, our spirits touched sickness.

In the season of falling leaves, it is said, they arrived upon the sunrise side of our world. Our people became sick. Many nations perished, many children, also. They said they were "pure," but upon close examination by our Chiefs and our council, we learned that they were unclean.

Their Chief John (Winthrop) also said they were "pure." Chief John spoke to those who were "pure," saying that they must bind all together as but a single being, and that their bindings must be their love for each other and their love for God--that in this manner they would prosper.

In this manner, Chief John said, they would grow many upon the land. He spoke saying that they would build a shining village upon the hill and their light would never, as the evening sun, fade into shadows. Chief John and God commanded. The "pure" followed every word.

They saw this land as a beautiful place created for them alone by their God, but they were not created here...The council spoke saying that this cannot be. The council said that they are intruding and wished for them to depart.

...And they did, they multiplied. It has been the passing of as many winters as there are fingers upon a hundred hands. They grew into many people upon this land--more than the leaves of the forest. It is true that have a good life issued to them by their invisible God. It is true they have built many shining villages-- one upon every hill they approached.

But, there is a truth spoken at the council fire in the softness of evening. Our Chief-Of-The-Council said: "It is true that the eastern people have grown many. It is true they have much land and many possessions. It is true they have made huge laws. It is true that they made shining villages upon the thousand hills. But they do not have happiness. They shall never find happiness for all of the seasons they worship The-God-Who-Cannot-Smile."

* Dates on Aztec/Mayan calendar.

Sincerely,

Darryl Babe Wilson
(Pit River)

Dear Christopher:

"In fourteen hundred and ninety-two Columbus sailed the ocean." I remember those words being ritualistically chanted by a white elementary school teacher as I grew up. I now watch my children bring home pictures glorifying the "Nina", "Pinta", and "Santa Maria" while attempting to compose in my mind the proper words to communicate my remorse at the denial of the truth of the history of our people, both red and white. I have suffered the loss of much of the richness of my Indian heritage at the hands of an assimilationist legacy. I attempt to teach my children about Indian culture today at the same time the public school system teaches them that Indian culture no longer exists. In my attempt to enlighten my children I encounter the attitude of "mom's on her Indian thing again"; but I am not giving up. I want my children to learn as much as possible of their Indian heritage, in spite of society's attempts to destroy our "savage ways".

I will continue to discuss error in the materials sent home with my children by well-meaning teachers, as well as by other teachers simply paying lip-service to multi-cultural curriculum. I will do so, even at the protests of my children who do not want their mother labelled as a trouble-maker. I feel sad when my children are taught that the greatest contribution of Indians to this nation is corn. What about the use of the Iroquois Nation's governmental structure as a model for the Articles of Confederation? I feel angry when the sweat lodge ceremonies are reduced to bathing. I become infuriated at the idea that the reverence and respect that Indians have for land has been replaced with the dominant society's "harnessing, exploiting, and controlling, attitude" toward the land: the attitude that becomes a "destroying" attitude if a profit can be turned. When my child angrily says " I am ashamed of the part of me that is white!", I feel that I have gotten through to some extent. However, I do not want her to be ashamed of any part of herself in order to realize the grave injustices that have been done and are being done to Indians.

I see Indians saying "No more to white ways!" These ways have deliberately attempted to annihilate a whole race. These ways have stolen sacred grounds and desecrated them. They have taken away the so-called primitive and inadequate social, political, religious, and economic structures that have provided a strong identity, justice, meaning to life, and subsistence for centuries. You shared the discovery of what you called an "artless and generous" people and laid the groundwork for the present system of colonization that befell the first people of this continent.

Indians presently request that the United States honor treaty agreements and acknowledge Indian sovereignty. The United States responds by silencing truth and forcing Indians to falsely testify against their brothers. The United States responds by using an impartial and color-blind justice system to imprison innocent Indian people with blatant false testimony. The United States responds by sending FBI agents to kill Indians who are willing to stand up to unrighteousness. The United States responds by contaminating Indian land, the same land that is relied upon for livelihood.

I grew up in this "great nation" created by "our" forefathers. Whose forefathers, I ask? I witnessed, through the media, the first man on the moon. I have utilized the result of various modern technologies in the form of microwaves and computers. I remember giggling in pure delight at my first experience with a word processor.

No thank you, Christopher, I do not honor you. I do not celebrate your arrival. We could have done without your metal pots and pans, the wheel and the horse. The price was too great.

Sincerely,

Loretta I. Winters
(Mississauga)

Dear Christopher:

I am writing this letter as a means to update you in reference to the backlash you have caused in my country. I call it "my country" because we are true Native Americans and have lived here for over 50 thousand years...

You're probably wondering why I am writing. The answer is quite simple, because I can write! When you first landed in my country, there was no way we could intelligently communicate. Therefore you called my people stupid, heathens, savages and much more. But now that I can write, there are many thoughts I would like to share with you. First I am a Member of the Osage Tribe of Indians, which is a branch of the Southern Sioux. Our tribal name before the white man came was (Wah-sha-she). If one were to trace the aboriginal name from Wah-sha-she, you would discover the name was (Ni-u-Kon-ska) which means freely, Children of the Middle Waters. The white man has given our tribe the name Osage; however most true tribe members prefer Wah-sha-she.

We were not the so called heathens or savages that you thought we were, far from it. At the time you arrived to our shores we had no need for the written word. Our communication was our tribal language. Our language was used by our tribe exclusively, and by other tribes located in areas of relationship. All tribes across our country could communicate by international hand-sign. Therefore we were able to communicate a multitude of different dialects. If urgency was a factor, where it was required to communicate at a great distance, we would utilize the drum, smoke, sun reflection, or runners to deliver the desired message. However, because you could not communicate with my people, you called them stupid! Please remember, it was you who missed the continent of India by thousands of miles and landed in my country. So

Dear Christopher

I ask...who was really the stupid one...? But great thinking, you called us Indians!

Your arrival to our land is now history and had it not been you, then it was only a matter of time before some other explorers would have made the discovery. Therefore it is hard to blame anyone for the inevitable. We greatly admire anyone who would bodily sail into uncharted worlds fearlessly and ready to face and to battle with the mythical hazards of the deep. However we do not admire you for the rape and plunder of our people and our lands! You and those who have followed are guilty. You were guilty then and you are guilty now. Time has passed but your crimes remain and continue, as there is no less difference between you and the present day congress. The bond between the two is still the same, money... Even to this day I hear the same old cliches; "You can't stop progress", "The whites are God's people", "The treaties were just", and etc. and etc. Was it justice to march into our camps with superior forces and to spread fire and desolation whenever you pleased? Was it justice to destroy our civilization, then try to make us adopt your strange laws, your religion, your manners and your customs? We do not see the propriety of such a reformation. You ask, "Why won't the Indian farm as we do?" May we ask with equal propriety, "Why do not the white people hunt and live as we do?"

The Great Spirit has placed us in different situations. He has given you many advantages, but he has not created us to be your slaves. We are a separate people! He has stocked your lands with cows, ours with buffalo; yours with hogs, ours with bears; yours with sheep, ours with deer. He has given you the advantage that your animals are tame, while ours are wild and demand not only a larger space for range, but to hunt and kill them. They are, nevertheless, as yours, and ought not to be taken from us without our consent, or for something of equal value. And of course this would include fish from all rivers and lakes. I don't wish to sound paranoid in reference to our government. However I only know what history has taught me, which is, the white government never meant to be fair with our Indian tribes, then or now! As an example the following brief selections are short segments from documented Presidential papers on file at Washington, D.C.

President Thomas Jefferson, 1803, writing a white viewpoint in reference to Indian tribes: "I consider the business of hunting has already become insufficient to furnish clothing and subsistence to the Indians. The promotion of agriculture, therefore, and household manufacture, are essential in there [sic] preservation, and I am disposed to aid and encourage it. This will enable them to live on much smaller portions of land...while they are learning to do better on less land, our increasing numbers will be calling for more land."

General Andrew Jackson, 1817, part of his letter to President Monroe: "It may be asked how this land is to be obtained from the Indians, they having refused to relinquish their claim to the commissioners lately appointed and authorized to this purchase from them. I have lone [long] viewed treaties with the Indians an absurdity not to be reconciled to the principles of government. The Indians are the subjects of the United States, inhabiting its territory and acknowledging it sovereignty, then is it not absurd for the sovereign to negotiate by treaty with the subject? I have always thought, that congress had as much right to regulate by acts of legislation, all Indian concerns, as they had of territories; there is only this difference, that the inhabitants of territories, are citizens of the United States and entitled to all the rights thereof; the Indians are subjects and entitled to their protection and fostering care is the legislature of the Union."

Dear Christopher

President James Monroe, 1825, in a message to Congress: "Being deeply impressed with the opinion, that the removal of the Indian Tribes from the limits of the several States and Territories, to the country lying westward and northward thereof, within our own acknowledged boundaries, is of very high importance to our Union, and may be accomplished on conditions, and in a manner, to promote the interest and happiness of those tribes, the attention has been drawn, with great solicitude, to the object. The United States are bound to extinguish the Indian title to the lands within it, whenever it may be done peaceably and on reasonable conditions. Experience has clearly demonstrated, that in their present state, it is impossible to incorporate them, in such masses, in any form whatever, into our system."

The Tribes were relocated and moved to the frontier. Treaties were made and broken by Congress. If Indian land was required by the white man, all that was needed was an unscrupulous politician, who could be hired for a vote or for money. Many people from the eastern States started moving westward in mass humanity. The Osage as well as other tribes were helpless against the diseases the white man was bringing, which were spreading like a prairie-fire, [by] which my tribe was almost reduced by half. Then the Osage were forced to sign treaties they did not understand. Again false promises by the U.S. Government! Osage treaties that were given to our tribe were taken away even faster. The following treaties are listed as an example:

Osage Treaty of 1808: Our tribe was forced to sign away most of Missouri and more than half of Arkansas.
Osage Treaty of 1818: Again forced to sign away our land in Oklahoma and Arkansas.
Osage Treaty of 1825: Forced to sign away our land in Kansas and over half the state of Oklahoma.
Treaty of 1808, ceded lands........... 50,000,000 acres

Dear Christopher

Treaty of 1818, ceded lands............ 1,800,000 acres

Treaty of 1825, ceded lands........... 96,800,000 acres

The Osages, in the Treaties of 1808, 1818, and 1825, ceded approximately 100,000,000 (million) acres to the U.S. Government. Our tribe received as compensation for this cession $166,300 in cash, annuities, livestock, horses, farming equipment and merchandise. Most of this was absorbed back into the white man's world. Christopher, to reduce the above numbers in reference to payment to our tribe, it represents one penny for each six acres ceded!

It was not only the Osage who were cheated out of their land. It was all tribes. Although I am an Osage tribe member, I also have relations from other tribes. My Great Great Grandfather, was a member of the Cherokee Tribe. His name was John Martin. The population of the Cherokee tribe by the enumeration of their agent in 1809 was 12,395 Cherokee, half of whom were of mixed blood; besides 585 Negro slaves, and 341 whites, making a total of 13,319. By 1820 they had increased to 14,500. They had property in horses, cattle, sheep, ploughs, mills, etc., estimated at about $571,500. Their country included at that time sixty-five villages and towns.

By 1825 their census showed a total population of 15,160, including 1,377 Negro slaves; they had 22,531 black cattle, 7,683 horses, 46,732 swine, 2,566 sheep, 330 goats, 762 looms, 2,486 spinning wheels, 172 wagons, 2,843 plows, 10 sawmills, 31 gristmills, one powder mill, 62 blacksmith shops, 8 cotton gins, 18 schools, 2 turnpikes, 18 ferries and 20 public roads.

On predatory excursions to the Carolinas, the Cherokees carried off slaves whom they used to work their lands, of whom 610 were males and 667 females. Their agricultural and industrial wealth consisted of 33 flour-mills, 13 sawmills, 69 forges, 2 tanneries, and other belongings of an industrious and progressive people.

On June 1, 1827 the Cherokee people held an election for delegates to a convention that was to form a constitution for the nation. The names of the districts were Chickamaugre, Coosewatte, Amaoah, Challoogee, Hickory Log, Etowah, Tanquohee, and Aquahee. The delegates from the first district were John Ross, Richard Taylor, and John Bainbridge; for the second district my Grandfather John Martin, Joseph Vann, and Kalachulee; from the third were Lewis Ross, Thomas Foreman and The Hare. The convention met at New Echota, July 26, 1827, and adopted a republican constitution.

At a later date in the race for principal Chief of the tribe, John Ross was elected overwhelmingly. For the newly created post of adviser to the Chief, Major Ridge was elected. The major's previous position as speaker of the council was taken by Chief Going Snake. My Grandfather John Martin was then elected treasurer of the nation. Later he was sent to Washington to serve as a member on a treaty council. Then in 1828 John Martin became a judge. Chief John Ross moved to a plantation only a mile from Major Ridge's, to be near New Echota. He built a comfortable house on the Coosa River. His orchards were planted with all manner of fruit, and on his lawns were peacocks, symbols of his wealth and pride.

By February 21, 1828, the Cherokee tribe had acquired their own newspaper. It was called the Phoenix. It was printed in English and in Cherokee. It was the first newspaper ever printed by Indians, the [first] ever printed for them, the first ever printed, at least in large part, in an Indian language. A linguist once said that Cherokee was the most complicated language he had ever studied, that he had isolated 178 forms of the verb "to tie".

Boudinot was the editor of the Phoenix. The first editorial was a criticism of the white hunger for Cherokee land. Georgia, encouraged by success in removing the Creek Indians out of the state, was applying more pressure on the Cherokees. Then the Georgia Legislature passed a bill placing all lands in Georgia under Georgian judicial jurisdiction, which, as they interpreted it, included the Cherokee's territory. Also, in December 1828, they passed a resolution intended to be a warning, a testing of the waters: The resolution further said that Georgia will not use force to exercise her authority "unless compelled to do so".

In 1828, in the United States national election, Andrew Jackson won the presidency. Soon after he sent a message to a Georgia congressman: "Build a fire under them. When it gets hot enough, they'll move."

In 1837 it was said that the Cherokee were further advanced in agriculture than any other tribe. Those living in the western country had between 1,000 and 1,100 farms where they produced corn, oats, potatoes, beans, peas, pumpkins, and melons and raised horses, cattle and hogs; some of them had taken and filled contracts for the garrison at Fort Gibson and for subsisting immigrant Indians to the amount of $60,000.00. John Rogers, a native Cherokee, was manufacturing eighty bushels of salt a day at the Grand Saline on Grand River, then considered one of the greatest assets of the Cherokee Nation. Native traders were engaged in merchandising and transportation, others operated gristmills and sawmills of great importance to the tribe. Native Cherokee traders, guided by Kichai Indians, were seen as far from home as the Forks of the Brazos River in Texas on their way to the Comanche Indians with powder and lead to exchange for horses.

Many blacks, perhaps most living in the Cherokee nation, spoke and understood both Cherokee and English.

They therefore knew much about the developments taking place under the laws. For instance, they knew that even yet they were unable to vote, to hold office, to marry or make love to a Cherokee or a white, to sell whiskey, to own property in the nation. They had no right to counsel, to testify in court, to protect themselves physically, even if attacked. Removed from citizenship, without representation, denied freedom to leave, they had the stolen right to teach one another, provided they did it unobtrusively, the right to tell stories snatched from the Bible and to create stories and songs of their own.

In July 1829, an event took place that shook the Cherokee's confidence in their ability to control their lands. It was more startling than an earthquake or a killing flood. The first inkling of the news was, rumor recalled, that a young black slave found a peculiar looking stone and showed it to his white master, who showed alert interest at once. Where had the lad found it? The slave told him; the spot was east of New Echota by about thirty miles. Another rumor attributed the discovery to an Indian youth living on Ward Creek who sold his pebble to a white trader, a Yankee, who recognized it. Gold. For a generation, at least since 1804, the gold mined in the United States came from North Carolina, with twenty million dollar's worth mined to date; but this new strike lay predominantly south of the North Carolina border, and much of it was within the Cherokee Territory, within the boundaries of Georgia...

The autumn of 1829 continued the invasion of men and mules, followed by the ravishing of the streams and banks, followed by thefts and deals, lies and purchases. Gold miners were not proper neighbors. The Cherokee council met, shocked and diminished by events too large to grapple with. They evaded the problem, delayed. Finally, nothing was done in council about the miners or Georgia. Depend on national influences to force Georgia to relent, missionaries privately advised. Take no rash action yourselves, either against Georgia or the miners. It's too big a problem for piecemeal measures or for resolutions.

Several weeks later, on December 7, President Jackson sent to Congress his first message, and in it he endorsed the removal of Indians from eastern America, "voluntary, for it would be cruel and unjust to compel them to abandon the graves of their fathers and seek a home in a distant land". He mentioned particularly, specifically, the Cherokees. Georgia's claim for jurisdiction would be upheld by the United States now, as in the days when it was established by President Jefferson. If they did not move voluntarily, the Cherokees would have to accept absorption by the state. Georgia's legislature met in mid-December, a week after Jackson's address; the members were encouraged by the President's assurances.

The legislature acknowledged the critics, but it overcame any and all hesitation. It passed laws forbidding any Indian to engage "in digging for gold in said land, and taking therefrom great amounts of value, thereby appropriating riches to themselves which of right equally belong to ever [sic] other citizen of the state". They passed a law that further denied Indians rights in a court, declaring that an Indian cannot testify in a trial involving white men; that no Indian testimony was valid without at least two white witnesses; that no Indian contract was valid without at least two white witnesses. They voted through a bill making it unlawful "for any person or body of persons...to prevent, or deter any Indian, head man, chief, or warrior of said Nation...from selling or ceding to the United States, for the use of Georgia, the whole or any part of said territory". They passed a bill making it illegal for any person or body of persons to prevent, by force or threat, Cherokees from agreeing to emigrate or from moving to the West. They passed in this same bill a provision outlawing all meetings of the Cherokee council and all political assemblies of Indians in Georgia, except for purposes of ceding land.

The *Phoenix*, on May 29, 1830, reported that a certain Cherokee farmer was asked by whites to sell them his horses, and he refused. They turned the horses out of the corral. While the farmer chased after his animals, white men entered his house and beat his wife unconscious. Boudinot wrote, "Here is the secret. Full license to our oppressors, and every avenue of justice closed to us. Yes, this is the bitter cup prepared for us by a republican and religious government, we shall drink it to the very dregs."

The Choctaws, meanwhile, conceded. That very month they made known their willingness to to treat with the federal government, to sell their present lands and to move west. President Jackson handled the negotiation himself.

By 1836 President Jackson was in no mood for sentiment. Almost eight years of the presidency had left him weakened in health and lacking portions of his famous vengefulness. He was damn tired of the Indians, anyway. Take Sam Houston, the Tennessee Cherokee sonofabitch who was no president of the so-called Republic of Texas: "the Raven" was showing all the Cherokee traits of defiance, was telling the United States government what to do.

And here was John Ross back in Washington again; did he, Jackson wondered, now reside in Washington? Consider his last petition, a plea signed by babes in arms and dead Indians, almost everybody using an X. What the hell did a petition mean, signed by sixteen thousand Xes? Anyway, the question is settled. They have two years from the date of Senate ratification to go peacefully. Otherwise, they'll go by force. God help them if they diddle away that time and have to be taken west by the military.

In July 1838, General Scott awarded the contract to the Cherokee council to conduct the removal of all remaining Cherokees still in the east, to an area in the west known as "Indian Territory", later to be recognized in 1907, as the State of Oklahoma. The Cherokees would travel by land in parties of a thousand each. Appeals to use the river [rather] than the land routes were turned down! Questions about the advisability of such land travel in winter were also shunted aside. So the greater part of the tribe, refusing to remove voluntarily, were driven from their homes at the point of the bayonet, herded into concentration camps, and forced out of the country. A few thousand were taken west as prisoners on steamboats, but the great body of the tribe numbering more than 13,000 was brought in thirteen parties on overland journeys of from three to five months through Tennessee, Kentucky, Illinois, Missouri, and Arkansas to the Indian Territory. The hardship, suffering, and mortality to which these unhappy people were subjected were appalling.

No report was ever made of the number of Cherokees who died as the result of the removal. It was as if the Government did not wish to preserve any information touching the fearful cost to the helpless Indians of that tragic enterprise, and was but little interested in that phase of the subject. From the fragmentary official figures it appeared that more than 1,600 of those alone who removed under the direction of John Ross died on the journey. It is known that the rate of mortality was higher among the previously removed parties, whose suffering led to the proposition that the Cherokee officers be permitted to manage the remainder of the emigration. Hundreds died in the stockades, and the concentration camps, chiefly by reason of the confinement and the rations furnished them, flour and other provisions to which they were unaccustomed, and which they did not know how to prepare.

Hundreds of others died soon after their arrival in the Indian Territory from sickness and exposure on the journey. A very small percentage of the old and infirm, and the very young survived the hardships of that ghastly undertaking. It has been stated upon good authority based upon all available data, that over 4,000 Cherokee Indians died as the result of the removal. This blood path of mud and tears would become known as the "Trail of Tears".

Eleanor Nellie McDaniel Martin, my Great Grandmother, widow of the late Judge John Martin, went to Fayettesville, Arkansas, to visit her youngest daughter and several granddaughters who were students at Miss Sophia Sawyer's seminary, so popular with the Cherokee people. While there she contracted pneumonia and after an illness of a week, died on March 14, 1849 at the age of 56.

Christopher, at the present time, the Bureau of Indian Affairs defines its aims as follows:

1.	To create conditions under which the Indians will advance their social, economic and political adjustment to achieve a status comparable to that of their non-Indian neighbors.
2.	To encourage Indians and Indian tribes to assume an increasing measure of self-sufficiency.
3.	To terminate, at appropriate times, Federal supervision and services special to Indians.

In my opinion, the Bureau of Indian Affairs should seek attainment of the following related objectives:

1.	Maximum Indian economic self-sufficiency.

2.   Full participation of Indians in American life.

3.   Equal citizenship privileges and responsibilities for all Indians.

Christopher, this letter should bring you up to date in reference to the nightmare you started with the American Indians. I hope you are aware that I have only touched on the problems of two tribes, whereas there are literally hundreds of other tribes which have greatly suffered, and are still suffering. I can only wonder what might have been the destiny of my country and our visionary people, had you or others not discovered our land.

I will close this letter by verse in the attempt to share with you a greater insight into our Native American philosophy.

*   *   *   *

This anthology is our Native American philosophy; the understanding of wisdom, dignity and pride.
Not to interpret the cosmos, but rather to acknowledge the value
Of strength from our Spiritual aide.

Our Spiritual strength has endured all afflictions, including the
travesty from the pony troop power.
But we have retained our ceremonies over the remnants of time, to
this day, and even to this hour.

In the beginning there was only the Life Mystery to be learned;
and as our knowledge grew,

So did our love for all creation, including the Great Spirit, and
the sacred Circle of virtue.

The Circle becomes charged with the sacred truth, and the giving of all life and power.
The Great Spirit is within all things; the animals the trees, the grass and the wild flower.

Pleasing it looked, this newly created world, along the entire length and breadth of the earth.
Our Grandmother extended the green reflection of her covering, while pleasant aromas gave birth.

Peace then comes within the soul when you realize the relationship within the Circle beyond,
There are no lesser need [s] for cathedrals as the Great Spirit
of the universe will always respond.

There are no temples or shrines among us, save those of nature and sacred affairs.
Like the warmth of a evening camp-fire, or the breath of His Spirit upon southern airs.

Our faith, not formulated in creeds, nor forced upon any unwilling to receive,
Produces no preaching or persecution, nor scoffers, or atheists who do not believe.

The Great Spirit sketches out the path of life for all earthly
creatures to follow, where to go, and how one arrives.
But leaves all to find their own way to get there, to act independently according to nature and their lives.

From the moment of birth to the cosmos quest, or the chants from the gathered tribes,

There are no other rites more important than the ceremony of the
Pipe, which brings a reverence impossible to describe.

It arbitrated disputes where no man could speak untruth, after touching his lips to the Pipe.
It would promote peace, and re-affirm tribes, and no one dared to misuse this right.

Our Pipe is our Bible, the church, the visible links to the Spiritual world, where the smoke ascends in sacred prayer.
It is santified, consecrated and symbolizes morality, ethics, and the perfection of the Great Spirit who is everywhere.

Smoking the Pipe is our angelus, it dispatches grief, brings Peace, acts as our council and binds words as requested.
No spiritual sacred presence is possible or could be expected.

The simple form of the Pipe is fraught with symbolism, while the wooden stem stood for all growing things.
The stone bowl was for the rocks, the foundation of the earth, with attached eagle feathers from wings.

The winged eagles were messengers from the element of air, and looked down upon all earth.
Any fur or leather tongs were provided by animals, which the Great Spirit nurtured from birth.

The sacred smoke came from the dried leaves of the sumac, and the glowing coal was the spark of prayer.
Before smoking, the Pipe was held to all four directions, heaven
and earth, then a breath of smoke to the spirits everywhere.

We also believe in the power of Mother-Earth, and all that grows
on her, and that everything is holy and powerful.
Mother-Earth hears the call; she awakens; she feels the
breath of a new dawn, and all is good and plentyful [sic].

The leaves and grass stir; all things move with the power that
governs everything; everywhere life is renewed this way.
How very mysterious; we are speaking of something very Sacred,
although it happens every day.

We were put on this world to learn of ourselves, and all
Spiritual law for the living.
We have learned that our laws have always remained,
while the White law does more taking than giving.

We do not think the measure of civilization is how tall its
buildings of concrete stand,
But rather how well its people have learned to integrate
environment and land.

All we asked were to be free men; free to talk and walk and
to travel our land.
Free to act for ourself, to follow our fathers' religion, and
to lead our children by their hand.

Our standards of conduct are just as rigid as the laws of
other people, as we live by the principles of honesty.
Absolute honesty towards each other is the basis of tribe
character, and the integrity of human modesty.

We find the power to articulate speech is not required to show
Superiority, as silence is more the keystone of the mind.
Profound silence and humility is the balance of the body,
while the conduct of patience is no more than time.

I seek strength, not to be greater than my brother, but to fight my greatest enemy...myself, to be without shame.
So when life fades, as the fading sunset, my soul may come to you (Great Spirit) without blame.

What is life? It is the flash of a firefly in the night, and the breath of a buffalo in wintertime.
It is the little shadow which runs across the grass, and loses itself in the sunset in springtime.

The Great Circle is timeless, like the question of destiny, or the purpose for human existence.
It is not life, but death, which goads us to seek the joy of being alive; and death that inspires the Circle of resistance.

But when death is imminent and darkness begins to fall, and you are living in the shadow of death,
You will never be more totally aware and alive as in the act of dying, and the sigh of your last breath.

During passover, your mind becomes crystal clear with heightened senses of perception,
This is the harmony of the endless Circle, the Circle of creation, the Circle of connection and resurrection.

Death is the separation of body and soul, the body enters the earthly citadel, the soul rises to a spiritual realm.
The soul then becomes unconstrained by time and space, while the spiritual hand commands the held.
Death is painless and only an interruption of life...not its end.

At night when the streets of your cities and villages are silent and you think them deserted, they will throng with the returning hosts that once filled them and still love this beautiful land. The White Man will never be alone.

Let him be just and deal kindly with my people, for the

dead are not powerless. Dead did I say? There is no death, only a change of worlds....

Sincerely,

Ronald Mossholder
(Osage)

Dear Christopher:

I've been working on this letter for some time now and it is, without a doubt, the most difficult letter I've ever written.

A lot of things have happened to the indigenous people of these lands since you first laid eyes on us almost five hundred years ago. I don't really hold you personally responsible for the many things and/or ways that the American Indian has suffered since your fateful journey in 1492, but since you have become a focal point for many of these issues of Native concern, I've taken this opportunity to address just one seemingly small area that just happened to be the reason for your trip in the first place.

I don't know if it's fair to say that you set the stage for future Anglo and Indian relations in the Americas, but you were among the first in a long line to use whatever means necessary to take what you came for. You came to our lands looking for gold, and when you found--through the assistance of Indians--what you sought, you wanted more and were willing to kill to get it. While you probably weren't the first, unfortunately you weren't the last. Since your own mission, Indians have been killed and removed from their homelands for everything from gold to better farmlands. And, as with you, anytime we were willing to compromise--to give even a little of the resources you and others sought--it only served to feed your greed. The fact is, your greed for gold and the greed others have had for these things could not possibly be worth what they cost you, Indian peoples, or the rest of the world.

You, dear Christopher, lost a lot more than you'll ever know. Did "discovering" a "new world" and attaining your riches lengthen your life on Earth? Did it earn you a place in heaven with the God in whose name you (and those who followed you) committed such atrocities? Would you not have attained the same fame and recognition--possibly even more so--if you had sought to know and understand these new peoples--think of the wonders you could then have offered your people back home through mutual respect and trade of not only the resources you sought but also of knowledge and information. But you did offer your people much, didn't you-- new land and resources--all tainted with the blood and anguish of people whose only mistake was to welcome you!

While it's obvious [that] European greed has cost Indians much: their land; livelihood; and all too often their lives; it's not so obvious what it cost the rest of the world. What the world has lost is the benefit of countless intelligent people who knew more about this land than is known today--even after five hundred years of "progression" and "educating" the "pagan" Indian. Puebloan peoples had an intricate irrigation system that allowed them to utilize land that to this day we consider to be barren. But for all of the scholars, philosophers, spiritual leaders, and great politicians this world lost through the virtual destruction of the Indian man, its biggest loss was the ability of Euroamericans to look any Indian--from the eldest to the youngest babe--in the eye, knowing that he and his people have given them at least the basic respect due to any living human being.

You can't be held responsible for anything other than your own actions, unfortunately, Chris, those actions are pretty damning in and of themselves. And even less fortunately, you weren't alone; too many more like you came along. It has been said that if it wasn't you then it would be someone else and this is true. The fact is that it was you and you set a very sad precedent--one that not only my people have had to suffer with, but your people as well. But the truth is, it is your people who have lost the most. They might have gold and land but we still retain our self respect and the knowledge that we have upheld our end of treaties and agreements made. A small number of your own people have been able to steal that right from your whole nation.

So, forgive me Chris, if, when some in this misled nation celebrate you on your day, I celebrate truly great people of the world--some Indian, some not, but all of them people who respect other people solely because they are people.

Sincerely,

Shawnlee Root
(Wasco/Tlingit)

Dear Christopher:

We are two Native American women, Blackfeet and Assiniboine, who relish the opportunity to write to you 500 years after your discovery paved the way for the European occupation of our lands.

Under the circumstances, our feelings towards you are not particularly negative. We believe that when you first landed on this continent, you were fulfilling a grand and daring vision. The land that you discovered was full of seemingly limitless potential. What a thrill it must have been for you to have made such a wonderful discovery. The people you met must also have seemed unique and beautiful, these brown-skinned people who became known as Indians because, we are told, you thought you were in India. However, we are aware that history can be altered to suit the views of those who write it. We see no more reason to reject the theory that the word "Indian" derived from your description of our ancestors as "In Dios", or "God's People", than to unequivocally accept that it was due to your error in geography.

The people known to you as Indians had a lot to share with you in the way of spirituality, methods of survival in this strange land, and a sense of respect for life. In return, you shared many valuable things with them. It might have been the beginning of a harmonious friendship in which both parties shared the beauty of a great land, and we wish it had been that way. Instead, we would like to tell you an unfortunate story about the land and the people that you found when you made your discovery of America. No--we are not bitter towards you, but we are angry at the exploitation and destruction that has been directed at both the land and its original inhabitants since your discovery.

Dear Christopher

The Indians that occupied this territory when you came here enjoyed the freedom of living on and utilizing the land as they saw fit. It was their right and their pleasure to do so. When the white people took over and set up their government, the Indians lost these privileges, which became increasingly smaller with the passage of time. According to history books, the country wasn't just taken from the Indians, it was purchased from them. The payments were accompanied by treaties said to be valid as long as the rivers flowed and the grass grew. In general the treaties promised that in return for the Indians' coveted land, the white people would ensure that the Indians had a place to live and a way to make a living. The natives then reserved parcels of land that their tribes would live on (reservations). Well Chris, the grass hasn't stopped growing and the water is still flowing; meanwhile the pittance we received for our land has long since been used up and the treaties that under the U.S. Constitution are "the law of the land' are treated by the white man as worthless as the paper they are written on.

Native Americans have been robbed of their vast tracts of land and are now trying to hold on to what little they have left. Recently the government has been trying to tax the land on the reservations, which in our opinion, is just another attempt to abolish the Indian way of life. It seems from the beginning that our people have been taken advantage of. We have been taught continually that our culture, vastly different from that of Europeans, is both inferior and undesirable. There are even those who would advocate the existence of a so-called pure white race, and demand that all those of other races go back to their native countries. Considering that this is our native land, we'd be happy if they were the first to act on their principles.

The native people of this country have not been the only victims since the coming of the Europeans. The environment too is in a big mess. As you probably remember, the Indian people valued and respected the land. Without the earth we could not have survived. There are people today who have raped this beautiful country for their own gain. Of course we realize that we have to utilize our natural resources in order to survive and to maintain a reasonable standard of living. Indian peoples believe that such resources should be appreciated and not taken for granted. If possible they should be allowed to regenerate, and at all costs prevented from extinction. Despite what may be called a low level of sophistication, Indian culture when it flourished, nevertheless managed to exist for thousands of years without upsetting the delicate balance of nature.

It seems the primary goal in peoples' lives nowadays is to make money, regardless of what you have to do to get it. Today we live in a society in which there are those who are incredibly rich and, despite there being enough to go around, those who are incredibly poor, so poor in fact that they are living on the street without food or shelter. Poor people get little help or sympathy from those who are well off, as poverty is viewed in almost all cases as being the result of laziness. This notion is proudly referred to as the American work ethic. If you are poor it is extremely hard to pull yourself up into a better situation. Things are set up for the convenience of those who are already rich and powerful. Indians unfortunately and naturally occupy a low rung in the ladder that is the white man's society. Indians, however, at least take care of their own. They respect and care for their old and young and would never think of neglecting or trashing them. There seems to be a lack of compassion and respect for human life in the white man's society. Is this news to you or were you white people always so brutal?

We sometimes wonder how things might have been if that great expedition of 1492 had never occurred, and we'd been left to progress at our own rate and in our own way. It is difficult to imagine, as we have grown up in an age of sophisticated technology, life without the material and time-saving comforts we have today. But instinctively, we feel that things would be better if we had been left to our own devices. Certainly we would still be able to hunt and fish wherever and whenever we pleased, and not have to worry about there not being enough game. We know that such diseases as smallpox, diabetes, and AIDS would never have run rampant. Our people would have been free from the ravages of alcoholism and endemic racism. There wouldn't be worries about toxic waste, of nuclear bombs, global warming or holes in the ozone layer. Our struggle would have been a simple one: to make the best living we could on the bountiful land given to us by God.

Naturally there are certain things we do to appreciate that came to us via the Europeans such as Mary Kay cosmetics, curling irons and the fact that we do not share our husbands with our sisters. We know this sounds like we'd like to have our cake and eat it too, and why not, white people do it every day. They enjoy the blessings of a large, productive continent, while its native peoples and rightful owners, those that have survived, occupy small barren corners here and there. Far from giving us what we are due, these invaders shrink from living up to the meagre promises they have tricked and bullied us into accepting. As far as they are concerned we as Indian peoples are at best tolerated, and generally a bother. They wish we'd go away so they can have the little we have left, and where possible they'll help us on our way.

We Indians--we are used to the name--supposedly have no feelings, and no self-respect, but we not about to give up the last vestiges of land and culture that remain, easily.

So now we hope you understand what was the legacy of your discovery, Chris. We believe that you were a man of noble vision and that one who so epitomized the adventurous, inquisitive spirit would never have intended that the dark-skinned people who greeted you welcomingly on the shores of our continent suffer such an ignominious decline. Yet here it is 500 years on. We can only offer you the benefit of the doubt, and the hope that in the future such intrepid ventures as yours are not the cause of such a meagre inheritance as ours.

Sincerely,

Janice Gordon
Karen Neumiller
(Blackfeet and Assiniboine)

Dear Christopher:

On this 500th anniversary of your discovery of America, we are writing to let you know that the world and the people you discovered are altered considerably since you set foot on the shores of Hispaniola. The people you discovered were not "Indians", and now we prefer to be called Native Americans and recognized as indigenous peoples and the rightful owners of the countries know known as the United States and Canada. Despite the mass destruction and genocide that came in the wake of your discovery, you are hearing 500 years later from two Blackfoot "Indians", one of many original nations that have survived despite the oppressive policies of every "foreign" government we have come into contact with.

We do not hold you personally responsible for all the evils that have been visited upon us in the past five centuries; however, neither are we appreciative of the fact that you brought a new kind of sophisticated savagery to our lands. Obviously you recognized that you possessed stronger military forces in setting out to claim our land for European powers and set the ball in motion for the events of the next 500 years with respect to the treatment of the original inhabitants of this continent.

The type of world view you brought to this country has from the very beginning allowed an oppression of native peoples and nations under the guise of moral and legal rationale. "Legally" we have been stripped of our lands and our cultures and it has all been justified morally. The fact that so many of us survive as distinct and recognizable at all is testament to our resiliency and our world view, both of which have remained intact. Our continued survival within a dominant government and dominant culture speaks loudly of the fact that we have been here longer, our culture and traditions are older and based on sounder principles of how the world and everything within it really works and what our role and our place is within the structure. Despite the fact that the two world views immediately collided, many "Indian" nations exist today in small areas of the United States called "Reservations" and retain remnants of self-government. We say "remnants" but mean that the types of governing bodies recognized by the United States do not resemble much our types of governing that fit in with our view of reality; they fit in with the dominant culture's view and were imposed supposedly to assist us in becoming self-governing in a manner acceptable to the larger society and thus are approved by the United States government and we are "allowed" to govern ourselves.

Along with the allowing, we are educated as other citizens of the United States and we learn side by side with non-Indians how to be good citizens of the USA. We also learn about the "savagery" of the original inhabitants of this country; how we scalped the poor white settlers and attacked those poor defenseless people when they settled on various parts of this country. We also learn how the United States "gave" us our Reservations and civilized us. We learn that our beliefs and our traditions were primitive and pagan. We are taught about how lazy, dumb, and dirty we are and, after the introduction of alcohol by non-Indians on first contact, we learn about what drunks we all are. And of course, the schools in which we are educated on reservations have lower standards than non-Indian schools because we are not capable of learning as much or as fast as other non-Indian citizens. When we attempt to attend a University, we are not equipped with the necessary skills and must attend classes that will provide the necessary skills and knowledge. But then again, special classes have to be provided to give us a view of ourselves that is more in line with our own views that have been passed down to us from our elders.

Nowhere in history books have we found ourselves without the bias of another opposing world view. So within we wrestle with judgements of ourselves based on standards by which we never measure up. Outwardly we may be brown and some of us even light skinned and we dress like other non-Indian citizens and even live in square houses but we are different inside and we crave and treasure that distinctiveness.

It is surprising that we are still here, considering that there have been concerted and sustained efforts to do away with us. In fact, at one time (and maybe that mentality still prevails) non-Indians believed that "the only good Indian is a dead Indian". Of course, these days the efforts to extinguish us are much more subtle but from our experience, not less savage. As we mentioned above, we live on reservations (small areas of land, minute compared to the original area) and in the past century were deprived of our abilities and our sustenance and placed in a dependent position. We received rations of food and clothing and blankets from the United States within the confines of our reservations and if we did not receive them, we starved and froze to death. We have always believed, because we learned in school, that the United States "gave" them to us. In fact, those rations were paid for by us when we ceded away large tracts of our original lands through treaties with the United States. If we starved and froze to death at any given time, it was because there were many greedy people responsible for the distribution of said items. After the need for more land to be obtained legally passed, efforts were made and are continuing to be made to obtain the reservation land by any means possible. Making the reservations uninhabitable is one method used to obtain more land. Reservations are pockets of poverty, unemployment and hopelessness due to lack of development of the people and the reservations' rich resources that has been deliberate, we believe, as a means to drive the people away from the reservations and leave the land to non-Indians who have been eyeing them with covetous eyes.

We guess it is no wonder we learn nothing about ourselves in the history book: the facts are so shameful especially the fact that the sophisticated savagery you brought to this country is alive and flourishing. You might be interested to know about the rest of the population of this country and the technological advances made just in the last century but we will leave it to others to inform you.

You will be proud to know that this country has set aside one day a year to celebrate your discovery and that many celebrations are planned in your honor in 1992. We do not find anything to celebrate about.

We do not mean to be rude, but what do you think we could possibly feel after 500 years of sophisticated savagery?

Sincerely,

Mary Gordon Sellers
David Gordon
(Blackfeet)

Dear Christopher:

On the 500th anniversary of your "invasion" into our country, we would just like to share with you a few thoughts.

Our first point would be that contrary to popular belief, you did not "discover" America. On the contrary, you discovered a land that was long in existence before your arrival and was inhabited by an indigenous people who you ironically named Indians. We still wonder how a person/country can discover something that was already inhabited?

Well Chris, "we" are the inheritors of the legacy that you discovered. "We" are told that "we" should be thankful to you for bringing us your European influences; your Christianity, your diseases, saving us from our own heathen ways. Well Chris, "we" have a surprise for you! We are not thankful for anything you brought us. Our people were doing just fine before your arrival upon our beaches.

We carried on our own traditions and cultures, despite your views as to our heathen beliefs and practices; we did have our own religions, we believed in our own Gods. We may not have prayed the same way you did, but we practiced our own religions which were passed onto us by our ancestor's oral traditions.

Let us just suppose for a time, that European invaders hadn't brought on their influences into this country. Let us suppose that these invaders allowed the Native Americans to keep their cultures, traditions, and allowed these people to hold onto their simple diets. Let us suppose that they even allowed these indigenous peoples to use their own natural medicines and continue using their own methods of communication and dress. Would that have been so bad?

Our Great-Great-Grandparents faced many hardships trying to hold onto what little they had of their own culture and religion. They were punished severely for speaking their own languages and punished for trying to practice their own religions. This led to a people who lost their identity and many lost the will to carry on their oral traditions. Can you imagine Chris, what it must feel like to lose part of your soul and an inner feeling of hopelessness?

We still hear our tribal elders speak of the government schools and the strict teachings they endured. For our elders there was no way out; it was "do as we say, or your people will cease to exist." It must have been hard for our ancestors to accept the new White man's way: to go from a proud, strong race of people, to a repressed, dependent people.

There are many books written on the Native American, from a White man's perspective, on how these people lost their cultures and traditions. We as Native Americans feel that no one can really feel how another feels in their hearts. We are a people of oral tradition and the loss of our culture can never be expressed by us or by any historian or so called cultural specialist.

There have been thousands of articles and books written about you, Chris, to date. This being the 500th anniversary of the year 1492, you are the most controversial person of 1992. We have read many articles about how the Native American should be thankful to you for bringing us your Christianity. We read articles that deemed us a lost land of "lost souls" before we were introduced to Christianity.

We have a few speculations on this point Chris, that maybe you can clear up for us.

Is it true that at one time you were deemed totally insane by your own peers and actually shipped back to Spain from Hispaniola in chains along with your brothers? Is it true that you refused to have the chains removed until you were granted a personal audience with the king and the queen and that your time was spent in a monastery in Selville, Spain, which ironically will be the host city of this year's World Fair, with a theme based upon your life and convictions? There are reports written that while you were in this monastery, you wrote a *Book of Prophecies* and that you believed that you had a calling to serve your White God and were sent to find the mines of Solomon in order to save the Holy City from the infidel and to prepare the way for the Messiah. In our other research, we found a statement by the Spanish sovereigns that their people were told to carry out evangelization by force, spreading the Christian religion by whatever means it took.

Then we came upon some really startling facts about you, Chris. It states that in actuality, you were considered a very barbaric person, who punished his own crew members by cutting off the tips of their noses and cutting off parts of their ears as punishment for stealing. This somehow doesn't fit into the "called to save his people" category.

The near extinction of your cultures and traditions brought on by Christianity, forced our ancestor to experience the most devastating era of our history.

Diseases were brought to the shores of the New World by the White man. These diseases were to become the downfall of the Native American. Our ancestors were a people who were totally unprepared to deal with these new diseases and sicknesses that they never had any contact [with] before.

All their medicines would do nothing to ward off the smallpox epidemics which were to kill their people by the thousands. The smallpox epidemic came first to the Blackfeet people in 1781, when a group of warriors attacked a village of Shoshone, not realizing that the village was in the midst of an epidemic. The Blackfeet warriors carried the virus to their villages to an unsuspecting tribe.

Alcohol was introduced to the Native Americans in 1794 during their many trading events. The Native Americans were encouraged to trade 30 or so beaver pelts for 1 large keg of what they called "Blackfoot Rum." It consisted of 4 to 5 quarts of pure alcohol and about 7 gallons of water, and the Native Americans didn't realize at that time that this was to become one of the Native Americans most epidemic/contagious diseases that we would have to endure.

Whooping cough also played a part in the infectious European-borne diseases introduced into Indian Country in 1819. This disease almost wiped out a third of the entire Blackfeet Nation.

In 1837 the smallpox again returned to haunt the Blackfeet people. The smallpox was spread by infected people and clothing that they traded for buffalo hides, again wiping out almost a third of their tribe. The smallpox would again hit the Blackfeet in 1845.

In 1864 scarlet fever hit the Blackfeet, killing about 1,000 or so people.

European diseases would continue to impact Native American people of all tribes for decades. These people had no chance to prepare for these mysterious sicknesses and had no ability to become immune to these diseases. As a consequence, thousands of our ancestors would die without really knowing where or when this sickness/disease was given to their people.

So you see Chris, your influences among the Native Americans and the effects you had on the Native American lies in your own history books. We only scratched the surface of what lies beneath the famous legacy of your "discovery" of America.

Native Americans have survived all the influences which you brought to our shores in the year 1492, and we will continue to survive the Eurocentric influences upon our lives every day. We are an indigenous people who have survived 500 years of your people pushing us off our own lands, bringing us your white man's diseases, taking away our ways of life, our cultures and our histories.

We have survived, Mr. Columbus, and we will continue to survive, because we believe that we were put upon this Earth for a purpose, and as Native Americans we will complete our circle of life and there are generations yet unborn that we are surviving for.

Sincerely,

Lewis W. Malatore
(Yakima/Cree)

Joseph G. Hamelin
(Blackfeet/Cree)

Marilyn Skahan-Malatore
(Yakima/Quinault)

Dear Christopher:

I have a story to tell you.

This is long, long ago, when the animals, plants, and people were in sync with one another and just about the time when you gave up the idea of following your father's tradition of weaving in favor of a crusade at sea. This was during the night when Oriole heard the night wind blowing gently. She heard the trees talking to one another. One of the redwood trees asked if another had heard about what the Loon doctor said about the whirligig beetle stealing the man's shadow. Another tree complained that the first tree had gotten things mixed up and it wasn't the Loon doctor who had said it, instead it was her *damaagomi,* her medicine, the Terrible Lizard, the one who lost all his children. The Terrible Lizard found this out because as a supernatural being he could go around listening to people talking without the people seeing him.

Later, the Hoot Owl was hunting and calling his mate. He asked if she had heard the news that it was a whirligig beetle who had stolen that sick man's shadow. And then he told her that this is what he had heard from the redwood trees who had been talking about it. With this news, Hoot Owl's mate hurried off to tell Mrs. Nighthawk.

And then when morning came, Bear felt better, but Loon Woman was still dizzy from her dream and she couldn't remember details. The others had to repeat to her everything that was said during her trance. At last she asked Bear if he could remember the place where he had seen that whirligig beetle.

And then when Bear assured her that he remembered the place, Loon Womon instructed him to go there and sing this whirligig song.

Whirligig Song

ph
-
-
m i

-
re
do

After Loon Woman sang the song four times, Bear said that he could remember it. And then Antelope volunteered how he agreed that Bear was a first class singer. Loon Woman said that the whirligig would come to the surface to see who was calling him when he heard the song. This was when Bear was supposed to ask for his shadow back. He was supposed to say firmly, "Mr. Whirligig, please give me back my shadow."

And then Loon Woman told Bear that he should do it, because Doctor Loon had Terrible Lizard for a hunting dog. As soon as he made the request, Bear was to turn around and return without turning his head or making any further comments. He was especially cautioned not to argue.

Bear left and while he was gone, the rest busied themselves around the camp. Loon Woman and Antelope sat together and talked. Loon took up baby Quail and sang a lullaby to her. The children were busy helping Grizzly to glue more sinews on the back of a bow. Coyote Old Man was making a bow-string. And then they all waited for Bear to come back with his shadow.

And then the story continues for hours recounting the Bear party and their travels to different countries where they encounter Grass People, Crane People, Flint People, Wild People, Porcupine, and more. Towards the end Oriole and Fox Boy are growing up into real people. This is where Fox was asking Oriole why they had grown up so fast when it only seemed like yesterday that they had begun their story and started to see the world with his father, who was then a real Bear. It was at this point that Oriole attempted to unravel the puzzle of whether Bear was a real Bear, only the beginning of a bear, a person-bear, a bearman, or a man-bear. From here the story continues and folds back onto itself in a lesson on the infinity of time.

So I was wondering, since you have the advantage of having hundreds of years of wandering around under your belt compared to my few, have you noticed if Bear found his shadow, because my theory is that things would begin to take better shape for Native peoples once that happens. The Loon Doctor told me and she heard it from the redwood trees who whisper in the night. That is, if I translated the Loon language correctly from my trance. This is where you come in, as an expert on Loon language. This would mean overlooking the definition of an "expert" as a has-been drip which is another story on the meaning of words.

Correct me I'm wrong, but wasn't it Loon language that you were using when you translated Arab nautical miles into Italian nautical miles a few centuries back?

On the other hand I may be mistaking it for Loon Logic. Either way, the information you can shed on the translation crisis I'm facing involving the subject of semiology will help us all in understanding Loon Logic in Loon Language. If you have a clue.
And this is the end of my story. Thank you.

Sincerely,

Sharon Manybeads Bowers
(Assiniboine/Haida/Chippewa)

Lushoot
Otterspace
Own-a-dragon
Nanowboosh
Wowbanowsky
Owl ribbon
Many-wampum
Ashbringer
Never-Strike
Smith

Dear Christopher:

As the Acting Secretary of the Northern Division of the Native Peoples' Pan-American Society, USA, I am writing to say that we have unanimously chosen you to receive our highest award: "Numero Uno First American White Man." We feel that this award for your genius in "discovering" us and introducing us to white man ways has been long overdue.

While we do by-pass the fact that other white men walked on these lands before you, and while we recognize that you did not drop anchor on our mainland (even after four attempts); nor did you, Sir "Admiral of the Ocean Sea," know precisely your global whereabouts (forever commemorating your geographical miscalculations by naming us "Indians"); nevertheless, the following reasons lead us to believe that you truly represent the white man as we have come to know him through five centuries.

First of all, your life has exemplified one of the bedrock tenets of American ideals: self-advancement. You knew how to get ahead in the world. You abandoned your Italian motherland for Portugal; cast off your Portuguese allegiance to sail under a Spanish flag; married into a family of political influence; conned a king and queen to outfit your ships; falsified the distance you sailed each day so that your sailors would not fear they had travelled so far from home; reneged on your promise to pay a reward to the first sailor who sighted land; and after returning from your first voyage with a few unknown plants, gold artifacts, and brown skinned natives (enslaved "in the name of Jesus"), you convinced the European world that you had indeed travelled to Marco Polo land by sailing west. Born of a seamstress and tavern keeper, you, Admiral, indeed fit the American Horatio Alger mold. No one can deny your pervasive feeling for political opportunism and pre-eminent yuppiehood.

And, your strongest driving force, the desire for gold, has foreshadowed today's American obsession with wealth. Forget those peaceful, friendly people whom you found, people whom you reported would make good Christians and "good servants." Forget those lush green islands of breath-taking beauty! No later than the day after landing, you wrote in your journal, "October 13:....So I resolved to go to the south-west to seek the gold and precious stones." And, "October 23: I did not delay longer here [on *Cabo del Isleo]* since I see that here there is no gold mine." And though you later did find gold (persuading the "unskilled in arms" natives to mine it for you), you never found the abundance of gold you sought. That bloody wealth fell to the conquistadores who followed you. But you showed the way. Slavery, rape, pillaging, genocide, and tribe-decimating diseases began with you.

And that legacy of fork-tongue reasoning and its resultant behavior has continued. Example:

The end justifies the means. (Which translated to "Kill the women and children, too." Nits make lice. And, "Slaughter the buffalo; let them injuns starve." And. "Injuns are gittin'cold; round up some smallpoxed blankets, men!")

Manifest Destiny. (Translation: "The white race is the super race; so, you redskins get out. The land is ours.")

All men are created equal. (The application of that theory has come to signify "Some men are created more equal" in the case of whites; and less equal in the case of Indians, blacks, Mexicans, and Asians.)

In God we trust. (These words utterly confused Native Americans because each group of white men appeared to puts its trust in a different God. Furthermore, the Indian God always came out a lesser God, no matter which group of white men was talking.)

As long as the grass shall grow. (When the white man concluded his treaties with those words, we saw that his fingers were crossed; but no one told us what that meant.)

The words and deeds go on ad infinitum.

So, Admiral of the Ocean Sea, in recognition of the legacy which you have left the native peoples on two continents, we sincerely bestow upon you the heart-felt title: "Numero Uno First American White Man."

Sincerely,

Glenn McGuire
(Pawnee)

Dear Christopher:

Many moons have passed since we stood on the shore
Waving to the people on ships going home.
Their gifts of pretty trinkets and pretty beads
I held close to my heart.
And their promises to return and stay with us
Working side by side.
They returned and brought others, so many more.
Until we felt closed in, trying to learn their way
Adaptation became impossible
They cleared much land, their buildings tall,
Monuments of their heroes standing in the midst
Of the stone wigwams that reach the sky.

I want to see the clouds but the stones are in my way
I want to walk the well-worn trails
But the stones hurt my moccassined feet.
I sweat in the closed spaces, my brow misty with memories
The picture on my mind a wigwam
With laughing children, my language spoken by everyone
My clothes are heavy, so different
I want to cry but that is not our way.
The gifts of pretty trinkets
And the pretty beads I hold
The promise still beating the heart
Why do I feel so alone?
I clutch the pretty beads and the trinkets.

Sincerely,

Rita Joe
(Micmac)

Dear Christopher:

In the last few years in this land that is called America by convention, there has been cause of jubilation and rhetoric on a job well done. These celebrations, with their parades and speeches, are said to owe their present life to you as the discoverer of this "New World."

To digress a bit, you *are* the person credited with finding the "New World" (America), hence you *are* the discoveror. This digression serves two purposes.

One: It shows how I, an Aboriginal of this land called America by convention (a Native), agree with the cultural norm that you, Christopher, *are!* the discoveror of America.

Two: More importantly the digression shows the distortion that facts can be put through to enhance a point of view, (As I am doing it will be said.).

First: From my point of view as an Aboriginal, my kinsman will call me a traitor for espousing the cultural norm that you are the discoveror of America; I will also be a traitor for not following the party line that goes something like this: "How can a person discover a land that already has millions of people living in it?" I will stand by the supposition that for *your* people *you* are the one who discovered America. This is the first distortion of facts--Christopher did and did not discover America, depending on whether you are an Aboriginal or an emigrant. And I am the traitor for relating reality. Aboriginals do not trust me because of what I say and emigrants do not trust me because I have apparently betrayed my own people.

Dear Christopher

Second: From the point of view of the Europeans, Did Christopher discover America or not?   If he did not discover America then a mechanism is needed to justify taking someone else's Life, Liberty and Property.   The simplest mechanism is to state that Christopher did discover America hence all he finds is his.   There are other mechanisms which basically dehumanize the Aboriginal inhabitants.   These dehumanizaztion techniques are much the same as reported by other minorities and political detainees.

Third: I wish to focus on the distortion that results when someone presents facts for consideration that are themselves distorted.   This results in a characterization of reality that the presenter wants us to see and not reality itself. From the book *Double-Speak* by William Lutz which gave us the "hexiform rotatable surface compression unit", a nut. We have a statement by Mr. Lutz, "One important function of doublespeak is to hide reality, to cover up what's really going on." (p. 171).   If I read Mr. Lutz correctly his statement and thesis (doublespeak) is a concise and easy to understand depiction of my third digression.

From my point of view today's quote/unquote controversy over your discovery of America is a *smokescreen* to cover up the real issue, which is: Your posterity is still on our land. Today's European American realize this, and so is still trying to justify himself and his presence here, hence even today (1992) he is still dehumanizing the Aboriginal peoples of America.   In the poem *Anchorage for Audre Lord* by Joy Harjo we are told the required out-come of our (Aboriginal) existence--

> "...Because who would believe
> the fantastic and terrible story of all
> of our survival
> those who were never meant
> to survive?"

--our continued existence and the European American's presence on our land is why the emigrant feels he must justify himself and dehumanise us.

I will explain the real problem to you, Mr. Columbus; there are as I see it two facets. *One:* We the Native People are still here. We have annihilated, we still possess a sense of cultural and national identity. *Two:* The descendents of non-aboriginal colonists have formed a culture and nation based on certain inalienable Rights that all mankind has been endowed with by his Creator. This is to say a culture and nation based on Truth and Justice, not one based on the power of the sword and/or terror.

In this second facet we see the seeds that gave birth to the self-actualization of the potential of mankind Vis-a-Vis his Creator; But also I see the seeds of death for mankind.

I see two facets on death here. *One:* The Nation the non-aboriginal colonists formed--called America or the U.S.A.--is so desirable as a way of life and as a Nation that other peoples, other cultures, and other Nations seek to emulate it. *Two:* As we the Native People are still here, are still around, then America must come to terms with us or moralize the basis of their Nation. When we combine these last two facets we have: (A) The possibility that we the Native People are finally annihilated: This act then, done by the emigrant Americans, is the death of America-- as the "certain inalienable Rights that all mankind has been endowed with by his Creator" are no longer valid. Or: (B) The other possibility is that we the Native People do not have...Rights...this act then--the denial of Rights and/or the politicalization of Rights--is the death of America.

We must keep in mind that America is a culture and a Nation based on "certain inalienable Rights that mankind has been endowed with by his Creator"; In 1992, Mr. Columbus, it is becoming more common to hear emigrants comment that it is too stifling, too bothersome to recognize the Basic Rights, hence America is coming closer to annihilation. And as mankind tends to emulate America, if America dies, so dies mankind.

A note, paradoxically as we the Aboriginal People are oppressed, at the very least not readily recognized as A People, so we to seek to emulate America--seek certain unalienable [sic] Rights. We have the "vision" of the founding fathers of America, as such I ask: "What do Americans of today (1992) have as a 'vision' "?

You see, Christopher, your children have done good and you have much to be proud of. I can only hope that they--America-- will choose to continue to recognize the basic rights that have been endowed to mankind by our Creator.

As it stands now, Christopher, the actions in procurement of the "European" title to the land, that is called the U.S.A., by your children were not accomplished in a manner that is legal by your children's procedures and rules of law. Even if the Native People had been annihilated, the facts (as seen by European Law) could not be changed so this part of the history of the U.S.A. would always haunt American culture and political life. **BUT!** your children did not annihilate the Native People so the "facts" are even harder to ignore.

So an attempt is made to ignore the facts, or an attempt is made to change the facts. There are many things that can be said about ignoring or changing the facts. The one thing that can be said is that it is an act of denial, in this case a denial of "facts". In this care that I write to you about, Christopher, I do not mean denial as in one person denying something from a second person. I mean **A** person denying something from **himself**. In this case denial is a denial of reality (or facts) by **A** person to **himself**. I am saying that reality is a fact and a fact is reality.

By European definition a denial of reality by someone is a mark of insanity. You see, Christopher, your children are insane. We can see that not only are your children insane but the culture and Nation they have formed is insane, it's possible for a Nation to be insane because in this case your children's Nation is based on certain "Rights" yet these very "Rights" are denied to the Native People of America. You see, Christopher, in this day and age a Nation is Laws and Laws are facts or reality and if reality (or facts) are denied than a case of insanity exists; So we have a world of people patterning themselves after a Nation that is insane. This is why I say I see the seeds of death for mankind.

People emigrate from their homeland to America for two reasons. The first is to escape hardship of some form in their homeland, usually economic or political. The second is to acquire the freedom to self-actualize, to be able to grow, to fulfill themselves. They also wish to acquire freedom for freedom's sake. In this instance I use the word "freedom" as a noun, this is the usual sense that is given to the concept "American Freedom". "American Freedom" is the simple and culturally normative way to say "(We have) certain unalienable Rights that all mankind have been endowed with by his Creator."

It could be said that I have no facts as to why people emigrate to America and/or that there are many more than only two reasons to emigrate. There is one fact, one instance of reality that I can describe for you, Christopher. This is the American Statue of Liberty. This statue is an icon, a cultural symbol, and in this case a symbol of Freedom.

This statue was given to America by France in 1884 as a token of friendship. It was also "a symbol of the liberty and brotherhood which the citizens of a country enjoy under a free form of government." from *The World Book Encyclopedia*, Vol 10, KL p. 4400, C. 1954. For more than one hundred years this statue has stood for liberty and freedom. There is a poem in the pedestal of the statue written [sic] by Emma Lazarus, part of the poem is:

> "Give me your tired, your poor,
> Your huddled masses yearning to
> breathe free,
> The wretched refuse of your teeming
> shore."

From this we see that America even offers freedom. This statue, this example of reality, is impossible to deny.

There are other examples of reality, other examples of "American Freedom" that are impossible to deny. I can not emphasize enough that to deny these foundations of America, these foundations of American Freedom, would be to unleash chaos on America, unleash chaos on the world.

Another example of fact when it comes to American Freedom is: "The Preamble" to "The Constitution of the United States of America". There are two parts to this example, Christopher. First, there are those who say that "The Preamble" has no weight, no significance to the constitution or to people, that it is just words--just posturing. This is true--The Creator will not send down a bolt of lightning to strike those people who ignore the preamble; Just as true the Creator will not harm those people who ignore the articles of the Constitution as well. In fact the Constitution could be deemed utter nonsense and voted null and void and the Creator will do nothing.

Now you might ask what is the force of the Constitution? And I will say the force of the Constitution is in the personal respect that people have for it; Thus the United States Constitution is an icon, a symbol of "Freedom", as well as a charter to govern conduct. It is in the symbol that is the Constitution that the Preamble has force.

To consider the Constitution as symbol and as charter, Mr. Columbus, we see that the "symbol" is reality and the "charter" is a description (imperfect as it may be of reality. Remembering Sir, that reality is a fact and a fact is reality, we consider again the "symbol". A symbol is a representation of a thing that all people will agree is the "thing"; For example my drawing [of a fish], people will say is a fish, or a symbol of a fish. Thus on further consideration a symbol *is* reality and "The Preamble" to "The Constitution of the United States of America" is reality.

Now we can consider the charter that is the Constitution. Most all people say that the Constitution has force because it is a charter. Let us look at this, Christopher. The Constitution does have power to direct individual behavior but also the individual can change the Constitution. An example of this is the 18th Amendment which prohibited intoxicating beverages and the 21st Amendment which did away with the 18th Amendment. This means the Constitution has limited power over people; So! Which is more powerful, the preamble or the constitution? "The Preamble" regulates no individual conduct; as such there is no way to limit "The Preamble". As "The Preamble" cannot be limited it is all powerful, but the power is not physical it is spiritual in nature and is given by the individual. After all of the above, we again come to the individual and the denial of reality. What happens Christopher, when your children deny the Native People the freedom of their culture and their Nation? Your children physically deny something from Natives, But! even more importantly they are denying from themselves, reality. They are denying reality hence they are insane. The reality that is "The Preamble":

> "We the people of the United States, in order
> to form a more perfect union, establish justice,
> insure domestic tranquility, provide
> for the common defence, promote the
> general welfare,
> and secure the blessings of liberty to ourselves
> and our posterity, do ordain and establish this
> Constitution for the United States of America."

Out of all the examples of "American Freedom," my third and last example I wish to show you, Christopher, is the American Declaration of Independence. This is an official document of the United States of America, even though people will tell you that it has no force. Irregardless as to whether or not the document has force, it is an official document because without this declaration of the dissolving of political ties between peoples, the United States could not have begun.

The only force the Declaration has as a charter is in defining the relations between people, and this definition is that no relations exist; Because the force, the charter, and the definition is negative, the duration of the Declaration is only instantaneous. To put it bluntly the Declaration was obsolete even as it was being written, but the Declaration does have force as a symbol.

Remembering that symbols do not regulate conduct so can not be limited, hence are all powerful; The American Declaration of Independence then is all powerful, as this power is one of spirit that is given by the people to the document. The entire document that is the Declaration is the epitome of "American Freedom". The passage from the document that is the symbol that everyone recognizes is:

"We hold these truths to be self-evident,
that all men are created equal,
that they are endowed by their Creator with
certain inalienable Rights,
that among these are Life, Liberty, and
the Pursuit of Happiness --That to
secure these Rights,
Governments are instituted among Men,
deriving their just Powers from the
consent of the governed.

Now that you have seen my examples you should be able to understand why you have much to be proud of, and you should be able to begin to grasp why you are a smoke screen. As I see it your children can do one of three things in regard to Natives: One) annihilate the Native People, Two) come to terms with the Native People, or Three) deny their symbols of American Freedom. All three options have been done in the last 500 years, in the last few years there has been less annihilation and denial and more consent being sought from Native People by emigrant Americans.

For example, in Alaska where I'm from an attempt at consent from Native People by your children was tried. This legislation, dealing with land issues, is called the Alaska Native Claims Settlement Act (ANCSA). This act has force as a charter but the symbol that it projects is not the symbol of "American Freedom". There are those who will say that ANCSA is the epitome of American Freedom but it is not. You see, Christopher, one of the "unalienable Rights" is that your claim against someone can not be judged by this same person or to put it more readably, no man can be the Judge at his own trial. In the case of Alaska Natives and emigrants, ANCSA is a judgement made against "The Judge" by "The Judge" hence ANCSA is not a symbol of "American Freedom". ANCSA is a smoke screen. ANCSA is a denial of reality, hence ANCSA is insane.

You see, Christopher, I pretty much have your children between a rock and a hard place; they just don't know it yet (ignorance is bliss), because I am not going to try to tell them what "American Freedom" is: Try to dictate my version of Reality, (Reality is fact and fact is Reality yet human interaction is consent). I will just ask is there "American Freedom" or not? The I will ask, do the Native Peoples have America have it yet?

Christopher, I am really a very mean and spiteful person, because I have placed your children in a very tight corner between a rock and a hard place; This corner is where your children must embrace Reality, or deny Reality. This corner is not my doing, I have no say in the matter; I only relate Reality as it has been taught to myself and the world by your children.

Out of spite I have one last and final example of "American Freedom" this is referred to as "The Rule of Law". This example is not a charter and it might not be a symbol as such; maybe it is all powerful. It can best be described as a theory or a rule of thumb. This theory is applied to all aspects of human interactions. In the case of Native People and your children, do all parties have it? Do all parties give it? Do all parties allow it?

This theory, the "the rule of law," was last used by your children's president (Bush). Mr. Bush stated at the United Nations Security Council meeting earlier this year that all Nations must obey "The Rule of Law" or face the consequences. This phrase "The Rule of Law" is the glue that binds all the charters and symbols together that allows existence to continue. So I ask, Christopher, does your child Bush obey "The Rule of Law", will he face the consequences of his actions, does he believe in any of the symbols of American Freedom?

To all of the above I say **No!** emphatically.

Sincerely,

Michael JH. Hormann
(Inupiaq)

Dear Christopher:

How touching and honouring it was for the whole world to see your living image on satellite television last night and for me, to be addressed by your personally, in my quality of first Supreme Chief of the newly recognized Indian Nation of America, on the occasion of the 500th anniversary of your landing in the "New World" (which, as you justly declared, was "just as old and civilized, in 1492, as your own 'Old World'".

This letter is to seek your very important moral support in a most special request dispatched yesterday (please find copy attached) by our government to the Prime Minister of India. My Council and myself recognize that our overture to the government of India corresponds in all major points to the declaration you made last night concerning the very sad fate of our People after your first arrival here in 1492.

Also, our government hereby expresses to you its wholehearted acceptance that you be present at our Nation's inaugural session at the Assembly of United Nations. In fact, we see your presence at that Session as a potent expression and a lasting symbol for the foremost goal we have committed ourselves to as a Nation: the attainment of genuine world unity around the Sacred Circle of Life honoured by our People, and of which you have spoken so convincingly to the world.

Lastly, we realize and accept, though with profound regret, that your time back here on Earth will not be a long one, as you have told the world, and for this reason, are looking forward to help make it as spiritually gratifying as possible. during your stay on what you have termed: "the Sacred Land of America".

Assured that this second meeting, five hundred years later, will be the true meeting of our hearts, minds and spirits, we are awaiting you, dear Christopher.

The Supreme Chief of the Indian Nation of America

*   *   *   *

Place of the First Peoples of America
United Nations Headquarters
Washington, D.C., 0004
U.S. of North America

Washington, D.C., October 12, 1992

His Excellency the Prime Minister of India
Legislative Assembly Building
New Delhi
India

Most honoured President:

First allow me to greet you in the name of the most newly recognized Nation on earth, the Indian Nation of America, of which I am the first Supreme Chief.

Last year, prior to the official declaration of the recognition of our Nation by the World Assembly of Nations, I had proposed to our National Council, of which I was the Vice-President, that our first official diplomatic gesture, of which the present letter is to reveal the subject to you, be directed to your Excellency. The National Council had then wholeheartedly accepted my proposition.

My Council and myself know full well that our overture will appear strange to your Excellency, but I shall say right from this moment that it is in no way any stranger than the fate which our People has known in direct relation with the reason for the request which is the subject of our overture.

Five hundred years ago today, an accident occurred that almost instantaneously changed the course of history, as well as the very description of the world as a whole: a European sailor named Christopher Columbus, found himself lost on the shores of our Continent.

That accident, as willed by the Great Power of the Universe, Master of all things, was a blessing for most other peoples of the world, but meant ruin and complete disaster for our ancestral Peoples.

I do not think it necessary, very dear President, to instruct you about the highly harmonious social and natural state in which the first peoples of America lived. I shall only say on this point that Christopher Columbus, as he himself said, had landed in an Earthly Paradise, which he took to be the Indies. Strangely, it never occurred to him then, any more [than he] cared to admit [to] any of his innumerable followers, that the land of riches which he was searching for was, in reality, poor in comparison with the one he "discovered".

To come closer to the subject of the present address, Christopher Columbus, and thereafter other Europeans who undertook to appropriate our Continent and to save our souls in the name of we know what (which produced the effects which we continue to know), named our land "Indies" and universally called its aboriginal inhabitants "Indians".

It is with the most authentic respect that we utilize this name, which we share with your people, knowing well that your country took a long time in learning about this history and becoming aware of the affliction of our peoples, and never helped in bringing it about.

Furthermore, we hope and we firmly believe that our Nation has never affronted the dignity, the sense for beauty and the capacity for Peace which the name *East Indians* has come to symbolize: for these virtues and qualities, the admiration of our people is forever yours.

Please allow me a few more remarks and explanations, dear President, before I unveil to you our request, which will also contain a proposal to your people, which you shall perchance accept.

Our Nation, all through these five hundred years, has lived, and continues to live a fundamentally demoralizing and weakening dilemma: that of existing without having a name of its own. I shall illustrate the gravity of this fact by explaining that by attaching a false name to our entire Nation, the oppressors created the notion that we did not have any right of existing, physically or culturally, in any part of our Continent. We were "Indians", consequently without rights, anywhere, in our own land.

Although we are rejoicing over the fact that the World Assembly of Nations has taken this decisive measure for our protection, we still are, dear brother President, after five centuries of constant exposure to all forms of aggression, a people without a name. One needs to have humaneness and compassion to understand the misfortune of a people so united by history, worldview and aspirations, but without a name to define and designate itself. Assuredly,, every Indian throughout history has felt this void and has attempted to imagine a name, a better name. No one, however, has been able to invent or discover a name truly apt to identify and signify the Nation.

Dear brother, the only name which, after all this time, has become natural to our minds and ears is the name *Indian*, and this is why that name, excepting the names of our loved ones and of our tribes, is to us the dearest sound that ever will be. It is probable that never a word has more characterized a people than that one. There is not a single contemporary inhabitant of our Continent who, upon hearing the word *Indian*, does not think about our people, and few who are not socially conditioned against us by some of the innumerable unfavorable preconceived ideas which this name evokes.

Brother, we most respectfully affirm that the name *Indian* has since long become more generally associated to our people than it is to yours. A proof of this is that if someone wants to refer to your people, he (she) must specify the origin by affixing the word "East"? to *Indian*, or else say: "from India". Besides, we are assured that inside the wide Asiatic world, it is more appropriate to refer to your people by a name belonging to a dominant language in your country and by which you should, in all logic, become universally known.

Dear brother President, the essence of our request is that your country officially make the gift of the name "Indian" to our newly recognized nameless Nation. This name, which we cherish and desire, would remain ours through a gift from your part, in memory of the hard fate known by our people during five centuries, and as a reminder of the essential moral values for the sake of which we have unconditionally resisted. This recognition, especially coming from your country, would leave a well-auguring mark, upon the birth of our Indian Nation of America and would also officially seal the already ancient, tacit alliance between our two Nations.

If this very special alliance between us should materialize, we would in our turn propose you to oblige us in the following way. The Indian Nation of America will establish preferential economic and political relations with your country, with the free access road to the common American world market which has thus far been closed to you. You and your trade partners of the so-called Third World shall have a first take in our resources available for trade; you shall be free to establish your diplomatic quarters in our cities and territories; the Indian Nation of America shall intervene against all and any racist or otherwise unjust manifestation reported by any member of your Alliance; The Indian Nation of America shall in all circumstances provide all possible material and moral support to the members of your Alliance, for as long as they shall not be engaged in war actions.

As I have suggested at the beginning of the present letter, our overture, however strange it may appear, is part of a process of correcting an act which still needs to be repaired and which, when examined in its original intent, appears infinitely stranger than the action which we are taking. Having said this, dear brother President, must I add that our Council, our Senate and myself are anxious to receive a reply from you?

In closing, may I request, dear President, that you transmit our fraternal greetings to the members of your government and to the people of India, when you submit to them the present overture? And whatever they should decide, tell them if you please, that we are waiting for the occasion to go and visit the people of the country which we have since long wished to see, and shall soon see.

May the Great Power of the Universe bless you and your people.

Sincerely,

Georges E. Sioui
(Huron-Wyandot)

Dear Christopher:

While the land of my heart and heritage is the Akwesasne Mohawk Nation, a place split in half by an arbitrary line demarking what is now called "the United States of America" and "Canada", and while the place I call home is New Mexico, I am writing to you from South America. I have worked in South America for about five of the last eight years (two in Africa) and feel I can fill you in on what is happening to a number of the remaining Native inhabitants whose lands you opened up to European incursion five centuries ago. My information comes from direct observation and from newspaper articles I have clipped during the last year or so (see bibliography). Even though somewhat superficial and telegraphic in form, I hope this report will be instructive. Direct translations will be in quotes, paraphrasing without quotes.

Let us start with the conclusion in a delicious display of non-Aristotelean logic:

"'No to tourism and colonization!' scream the indigenous communities", in a newspaper report. "The native communities are proclaiming their right to live in peace without the intervention of outsiders who are bent on conquering and colonizing the Federal Territory of Amazonas (in southern Venezuela)," say the Yanomami. The Piaroa community of Uhuottuja del Sipapo has authorized a spokesperson to deal with 'foreigners'. The slogan of the Piaroa organization is 'for life, land, sovereignty, language, religion and our own culture.'"

The report says that the tribes intend to go against the government's intentions to open up their homelands for tourism under the pretense that tourism will improve the welfare of the people when in fact it puts money into the hands only of middlemen and does nothing more than "alienate the land and sovereignty of all the natives of Venezuela and the Americas....The promotion of tourism is one and the same thing,--a new land occupation of the Amazon area by strangers, ignoring the native communities and even the mixed-bloods settled there," according to the Council of Elders. They listed the reasons why tourism is anathema to native communities: 1) it displaces natives in order to promote new kinds of occupation of the land by outsiders, i.e., colonization; 2) it destroys or destabilizes the native economic system; 3) it breaks the environmental equilibrium; 4) it provokes internal upheaval and ethnocide by means of family disintegration, the proliferation of diseases of all kinds coming in from outside, alcoholism, prostitution, and drugs; and 5) cultural genocide and, ultimately, the final physical destruction of the people."

The Council of Elders urges two additional observances. The elders believe that native heroes deserve to be immortalized in national places such as in the halls of Congress, the Tomb of the Unknowns, Mount Rushmore-kinds of monuments, and the like, celebrated as patriot chiefs on the same footing as European-Americans who now fill all such publicly-hallowed grounds. And finally, they reject categorically all the euphemistic terminology used as cover-ups for the five-century old event, terms like: "The Discovery", "The Day of the (Hispanic) Race - *Dia de la Raza,* " the "Encounter of Two Worlds," "Encounter of Two Hemispheres," etc. which intend to make light of the dark and sad history resulting from the Conquest of America. (1)

The following newspaper clips will give you a sense of day-to-day problems with which the Native communities in Latin America are struggling. References will be found at the end of the list.

Dear Christopher

INVOLUNTARY RELOCATION

Members of the Guajiro Tribe are being taken from their homes on the arid Guajira Peninsula, Venezuela, to work on farms and in coal mines in the southern part of Aragua State under "inhumane conditions, in barracks without light or water or any sanitary means", conditions ripe for the invasion of cholera, now being investigated by authorities. (2)

There is a plan by the Chilean government to build as many as six dams along the Bio-Bio, one of Chile's largest rivers, whose crystalline waters run through the lands of the isolated Pehuenche tribe. "The dams will be the end of Pehuenche life," said Mrs. Huenchucan. "We don't trust these people. Yes, we are poor, but we want to live as we have always lived, with the old customs of our ancestors. We want our children to speak our language. The dam will ruin that."

Though they were a nomadic people for hundreds of years, a half century ago the government allocated large tracts of land along the 80 miles of the Bio-Bio to the Pehuenches, one of five major Indian groups in Chile, with a total population of more than 600,000. The rough terrain has so isolated the Pehuenches that until recently they were almost unknown outside the region. (3)

The governor of Caracas, Antonio Ledezma, drew attention to the practice of enticing Indians from the countryside to come work in the cities for which they are totally unprepared. He warned of strong sanctions and heavy fines for those who are transporting them into the cities, and will hold the municipal and district authorities responsible for any more of this activity. (4)

Dear Christopher

LAND REFORM AND POLITICAL RIGHTS

Ecuador: "A war of words is daily front-page news" in Quito where the large Indian population is in a "collision course with the government and large landowners--a course both sides warn could lead to violence. Ecuador could be the next target of insurrectionist groups such as Peru's Shining Path, which has combined radical Maoism with calls for restoration of Indian supremacy". At the heart of the conflict is the demand of the National Confederation of Indigenous Nations of Ecuador that the government grant land and special sovereignty to Indians, including mineral and oil rights. The group also is demanding radical land reform under the slogan 'not one hacienda (large land holding) left by '92', in part to protest celebrations of the 500th anniversary of the Spanish discovery of the New World." Estimates of the size of the Indian population range from 25 to 40 percent of Ecuador's total of 10 million, the majority of which is mestizo, or mixed-race.

Most Indians are highland Quechuas, but the Indian confederation also includes other highland tribes as well as ethnic groups from the Amazon basin. In its first real test of strength, the Confederation mobilized more than 1 million people across the country on June 4 to blockade main highways, 'invade' private land and occupy churches in support of its demands. The protest's scope and coordination astounded much of the non-Indian population." In Ecuador, the indigenous people feel that they should not celebrate the arrival of Europeans some 500 hundred years ago but rather try to recover the lands taken from them. They confess they historically "accepted" Christianity but still believe that there are gods in the rivers, lakes, mountains and the sun for whom they give thanks for their lives and blessings. (5)

INVADERS OF INDIAN LANDS: Tourists, Garimpeiros
(gold and diamond hunters)_, Military Forces, Farmers,
Drug Growers/Traffickers, Missionaries, Guerillas,
Urbanization, Floral and Faunal Species Hunters,
Lumbering Interests, Famous Persons, Weapons
Purveyors, Adventurers, Scientists, Environmentalists,
Indian Lovers...

FIRST THE GOOD NEWS: Datelined Rio de Janeiro, the
Brazilian National Indian Foundation (FUNAI) has begun
to set the borders of a 94,000 square kilometer area, equal
to Austria in size, reserved exclusively for the 10,000
Yanomami Indians who live on the Brazilian side of the
Amazon.   An area of 45,000 has been demarked on the
Venezuelan side for the 12,000 Yanomamis there.

With the establishment of the Upper Orinoco-
Casiquiare Biosphere Reserve in which 15,000 Venezuelan
Yanomamis live, Naturalist Charles Brewer Carias is
guardedly pleased, saying "I am really worried that the
Yanomamis will not be protected by those who want to
Christianize them."   He and anthropologist Napoleon
Chagnon have proposed regulations to govern the area: a)
to limit the advancement of religious missionaries
beyond their current settlements, b) halt or inhibit the
Yanomami's access to weapons, including guns and
bullets, which enter the villages through contact with the
National Guard, the missions, and Christianized Indians,
c) relocate the military forts near the Brazilian border out
of Yanomami territory, d) create a program to control
epidemic spread for whooping cough, measles, chicken
pox, cholera, etc., and e) design an education system that
preserves the Yanomamis' traditional technical and
cultural values.   The only way to protect these people is to
protect them from us, our ailments, television--
everything which will completely devastate that group.
Our culture has nothing to give them." (6)

NOW FOR THE BAD NEWS: The Bari Indian community of the Sierra de Perija is facing a conflict in which the penetration of the Venezuelan petroleum industry and companies exploiting coal are reducing their holdings. A group of Bari travelled to Caracas to protest against the usurpation of their lands and the imminent destruction of their ecological and human territory. In Venezuela, the Bari number about 2,000 but there are others who live in Colombia as a result of having been pushed out of their homelands.

Since 1960 a progressive extermination of the Bari has occurred caused by confrontations with hired men from the large ranches and the petroleum companies who were paid for each pair of Bari ears that they could show as proof of the success of their 'hunting', according to Padre Jesue Garcia of the Capuchin Order. The Bari today are protesting against the ecological destruction and contamination brought about by mineral exploitation in which the trees are cut down or blown up by explosives, the rivers are poisoned and the fish which make up the major element in their diets are dying. (7)

The Bari Indians of the Perija area recently returned motors donated to them by the Venezuela petroleum company Maraven, because, they said, Maraven is continuing the political tradition of using cheap gifts to seduce the Indians. The position of their leaders is that their lands are not for sale nor can they be bought with money and gifts or motors. They decided to return the motors in a public ceremony to signify that they are not agreeing to the exploration of their territory by petroleum and coal companies. (8)

Religious sects and foreign tourists are invading the Piaroa Indian population in Sipapo in the Amazon, according to the National Indian Council of Venezuela and the Piaroa Indian Organization. They denounced a

Korean religious sect from Los Angeles, California which since 1989 has brought in tourists in their four airplanes and two launches to visit the Piaroa cemeteries and sacred temples where "they steal Indian bones and other objects to take as souvenirs." (9)

The Pemon are the Gran Sabana's major Indian tribe. Many of them live in remote, traditional villages or long thatched huts. Iona Nonato and her husband are park guards in Venezuela's enormous Canaiman National Park which encompasses their traditional homeland. "We are worried about the park," she says, "we wanted to be park guards to take care of everything, to watch over it. We feel everything that happens here. It hurts us to see what the tourists are doing to our homeland." (10)

The Piaroa Indians have charged the Governor of Amazon Territory with indiscriminate promotion of tourism, saying he has bought airplanes and boats carrying national and international tourists through their [cemeteries] where they profane their tombs and sacred temples, and take away the bones of their ancestors. (11)

In the Indian communities of the Yukpa they are continuing to construct a kind of war-prevention system against the threat of spill-over onto their lands of a nearby landowner who wants to take their lands from them. The landowner is using hired assassins from Colombia to commit aggressive acts and kill Yukpas. "Numerous tribes are running away from their lands in Sierra de Perija to avoid the invaders." Landowners accompanied by members of the National Guard violently attacked the Indian community of Aroy in Sierra de Perija during the weekend, and until now, it is not known what the results are nor the number of victims. The Yukpas are an ethnic group who have lived there since time immemorial, in a mountainous area that since 1968 was decreed a national park. The conflict began some 14 years ago when land seekers began invading the park and taking by force the best lands. At this time, the 3,000 Yukpas are facing outright war." (12)

In a new kind of cross-border migration, thousands of impoverished Brazilian garimpeiros--gold miners--have flooded into a recently created Yanomami Indian reserve in Venezuela's Amazon. Indian defenders assert that miners expose the long-isolated tribe to fatal diseases and to environmental degradation. Brazil's Indian protection service reports that in 1991, 180 Yanomami died of malaria and 17 died of yellow fever. (13)

At the Colombian headquarters of major rivers, there is an invasion going on by peasant farmers taking land, by drug growers and traffickers, and by armed guerillas. There are ancient communities of Indians in that area who are trying to get their lands back from the peasants when they had to flee in the 1950s. (14)

More than 60% of aboriginal communities in the world are threatened by urbanization. In this regard, the 4th International Congress of National Parks and Protected Areas explored how to develop and sustain parks while offering protection to the rural native communities which reside there. (15)

Illegal collectors of birds are selling macaws, parrots and song birds for high prices in three Orinoco river states. At the present time there are bands of unscrupulous men coming into the land of the Warao tribe, trapping birds for sale to dealers who send the birds on to Europe and the United States. (16)

Nicaragua has turned down a Taiwanese firm's logging proposal for 500,000 acres of rainforest in a victory for ecologists and a defeat for unemployed

Indians. The project would have created about 4,000 jobs in Central America's poorest country. (17)

"While in Venezuela, Sting may travel with Channel 2's Project Earth crew to the Amazon where he intends to shoot some short films on the Piaroa and Yanomami Indians." (18)

The Kari'nas Indian community demand the right to occupy lands they have owned since 1783 under title granted them by Charles III of Spain. In 1904 a law was passed establishing squatter rights to the territory whose Indians, it was believed, were "disappearing". Jose Poyo, leader of the group, indicated that "the 1904 law has kept us from farming our lands and all last year we were not able to plant our crops nor build houses, nor did we have anything to eat. By fact and right, these lands are ours, justice is on our side, and, we hope, so are the courts." (19)

Indignant over the celebrations of the 500th Century since the improperly called "Discovery of America", the Mapuche of Chile and Argentina, a Native tribe which never fell under the domination of the Spanish Crown during almost three centuries of bloody struggle which began in 1536, today announced their irrevocable decision to begin a massive process to recover almost ten million hectares of land usurped by the white man, starting in October. (20)

"Recently, during his tenure as president of Vemezuela, Jaime Lusinchi ignored a decision in which the Venezuelan Agrarian Institute had recognized the lands in the northeastern Grand Savannah area belonged to the Arecuna Indian nation. Lusinchi told a delegation of Arecunas that there were too few Indians for so much land. Actually, the Arecunas were just demanding that they be granted the same rights awarded other Venezuelans who had been authorized to build lodging facilities for tourists in the area reserved for Amerindians by the Agrarian Institute, something that was denied the Arecunas." (21)

The Colombian drug gangs are said to be organizing an expansion of coca plantations in the western state of Amazonas. The Brazilian Federal Indian Bureau says traffickers pay Amazon Indians to transport coca paste. (22)

The results of investigation over the last two years in the Alto Orinoco indicate the presence of firearms in the hands of Yanomami Indians who live close by the missionary settlements, according to Issam Madi, a sociologist. Some twenty-two Indians have been killed by firearms in the Yanomami communities which traditionally depend on bows and arrows for their defense and hunting and who have not till now had modern weapons. According to him, the missionaries are giving the Yanomami shotguns for hunting but the Indians are using them for warfare among their own groups. (23)

DISEASES, DEATH, ETC.: Datelined Santarem, Brazil, Dr. Fernando Branches, a physician, reports that "the international community is rightly worried about destruction of the rain forest. But the damage done by mercury will be a far more devastating environmental and human disaster." The element attacks the central nervous system and, in acute cases, can kill by causing kidney failure. The gold miners have dumped an estimated 1,500 tons of mercury into the Amazon which yields about 80 percent of Brazil's gold. Miners use mercury to bind with gold, filtering out silt and ore. They remove it with a blowtorch, a process repeated at trading posts before the gold is weighed for sale. When mercury is burned it releases a thick, white smoke, which enters the blood stream through the lungs, then spreads to the kidneys. "The delayed toxic effects of mercury could turn regions within the Amazon into tropical Minamatas, the bay where 1,000 deaths were caused by mercury poisoning," said biochemist Olaf Malme. (24)

Datelined Rio de Janiero, Brazil's National Indian Council Spokesman Eduardo Franklin reported that South America's cholera epidemic has hit Brazil's primitive Amazon Indians, and health experts said the fast-moving disease could devastate several defenseless tribes. At least 60,000 Indians could be infected within two months in the remote western jungle states. Cholera, a water-borne intestinal infection that causes vomiting and diarrhea, can kill a person in ten hours though it is easily treated with rehydration salts, intravenous fluids and antibiotics. But language differences, the remoteness of the Indian villages and the traditional tribal lifestyle make prevention among the Indians even more difficult, health officials say. (25)

In order to alert the inhabitants of the river regions where cholera is running its course, the Argentine government is transmitting health information in various languages to warn the Matacos, Chiguano, Tobas and Chorotes Tribes whose members have produced almost all of the cases of cholera to date. The government of Formosa Province, 1,300 kilometers north of Bueno Aires, confirmed that an Indian located at Mission Yacare in the far region of the Chaco has contracted cholera. Another nine victims live on the other side of this province where another major outbreak is expected. In Salta Province there are 194 cases to date of which 144 were found in Pilcomayo (along the Pilcomayo River which runs from Bolivia marking the frontier between the Argentine and Paraguayan Chaco). (26)

"While we had fascinating encounters with the Yanomami, explorer/adventurer De Bellard Pietri said that they suffered a terrible epidemic of malaria. 'It killed 104 of the Yanomami in the area where we were exploring and at least 41 of the 127 of the next group we were visiting were stricken by it. This was an extremely virulent strain that is resistant to all quinine-based medicine'." (27)

The native community of Paraujana and Guajira Indians of Laguna Sinamaica was struck by cholera recently. "They live in conditions of critical poverty, bad eating and health habits and unsanitary environments which make their habitat very precarious. (But) for cultural reasons, the Indians are resistant to changes in their lifestyles." (28)

A group of Indians, all of whom are relatives of traffic victims in accidents which occurred in the state of Zulia, took over the city bus station as a method to protest against the bus lines which refuse to take blame for the deaths. "We understand that up till now, the bus companies have taken no responsibility for damages in these cases." (29)

Problems in the Indian communities are caused by social pressures resulting in alcoholism, drug dependency and prostitution, maternal-infant health, tuberculosis, family violence, malnutrition and cholera. Jaime Clavet, a scientist in Lima, said that infant mortality in the Federal Amazon Territory is more than double that of the Venezuelan population elsewhere, diarrhea is the principle case of child death, and maternal deaths are four times the national rate. Malaria has increased in the Indian groups from 576 in 1980 to 4,974 in 1990. These changes in the health picture have been brought about by petroleum exploration, gold miners, military encampments, drug cultivation, the tourist industry, diamond miners and illegal lumbering companies. (30)

The "lost people, the sick people, the crazy people with broken thoughts"--that is, non-Indians--are threatening Davi Kopenawa Yanomami's world in the Brazilian rain forest, and he wants no part of them. "Leave us alone," is the message of this tribesman, who until recently knew nothing of clothing, numbers of the wheel. He asks for money to fight the diseases--malaria, tuberculosis, measles--that white prospectors (garimpeiros) have brought to the world's largest known primitive tribe. About 1,500 Brazilian Yanomamis have died from disease since the gold rush began in 1987; malaria rates are as high as 90 percent in some villages. "When I was a child, the missionaries brought measles, so many of our people died," Davi said. "Always the white people brought diseases to us." (31)

More than 40 Pemons and Kari'nas located in the Delta Amacuro Territory of Venezuela have died from measles, malaria and tuberculosis while authorities have done nothing to help. An official said that "the few survivors left have migrated out of the territory. National Guard helicopters have flown over the zone without seeing any of the surviving Indians to rescue." (32)

"The wave of suicides among young men on the Dourados reservation (some 3,000 hectares in the state of Mato Grosso South, Brazil) is because the Indians of the Kaiva, Terena and Guarani Tribes cannot stand white civilization, according to Alvaro, Orlando and Claudio Villas Boas who work with Brazil's native peoples. They said that the Indians are very attached to their tribal customs, they speak only their own language and prefer to kill themselves rather than suffer the presence of civilized man. Seventy-four males between 14 and 18 have committed suicide out of a total population of 3,600 during the last two years. (33)

Parasites, diarrhea and malnutrition attack half of the infants that live in the Delta Amacuro, the principle causes being the consumption of unclean water, deficient sanitary information, the deterioration or non-existence of sewage systems, and the lack of disease prevention programs. Additionally, there are other diseases attacking the children, including the common cold, respiratory diseases, bronchial asthma, pneumonia and pulmonary tuberculosis. (34)

RESERVED FOR WHAT? "The Tirio people, a tribe on the Brazil-Suriname border, use about 300 plants for medicine. The six or so shamans among the Tirio are all between 55 and 65, but the young people don't respect them. Not a single shaman has an apprentice. Furthermore, younger people often disdain local remedies in favor of newly available modern medicine. In Costa Rica, Conservation International convened a meeting of the medicine men of the Bibri Tribe toward the same end,- -to collect and save information about healing plants; similar efforts are planned for tribal communities in Colombia, Ecuador, Guyana And Suriname." (35)

"We hope to get basic information on plants used by the Yanomami." (36)

A report in "The Economist" which refers to unnamed physical anthropologists as the source indicated that a genetic bank has been proposed to house DNA samples from aboriginal groups in danger of extinction so that their characteristic DNA arrays can be saved for future study. Not only do the scientists lament the possibility that the remaining small groups will be erased from the face of the earth before their DNA can be collected and studied, but also that if there are survivors, the remaining ones will no longer be genetically pure due to intermixture with other gene pools. (37)

"There isn't a single visitor to this village who does not admire how this Amaicha Indian community is organized, now grown to some 4,600 families on 97,000 hectares of land, with an administrative center, tractors, trucks, agricultural machines, national and international telephone service, computers and a FAX machine. 'This is really admirable, an example of community life for all Argentinians to see'. The Amaicha del Valle Association buys what it needs communally in order to lower costs, principally on foodstuffs. They also bring in money from their arts and crafts coop which has contacts to sell their products both nationally and internationally." (38)

Admiral Colombus, some six inches of newsclips from two years of casual snipping remain in my file and will have to go unreported here. The above should, however, give you a sense of how things are. You will note that I threw in a few positive stories, although there aren't a lot of them. I failed to include reports of North Americans who are buying Native babies from poor Indian women in the Andean countries (CNN 03/10/92) and in Paraguay where I witnessed this myself. I failed to mention that Native populations are in the majority in six Latin American countries, and if one could look forward to the day when mestizos would identify with Indians rather than with European descendants, then it might be said that there is still a singular Indian presence *despite* five hundred years.

Bolivian historian Teresa Gisbert recently observed that "Latin America's marginality if intensified by the fact that the creole -- mixed-blood -- society in the years following independence from Spain has shown a notorious lack of understanding about the Indian part of their culture, and by denying its existence, has remained a society divided which will remain troubled...and indefinitely in a state of unrest. The positive side of the past has been this same biological and cultural mixing, showing the possibility of a dynamic and productive cultural florescence growing out of this marriage. (39)

While this is a rather long letter, Chris, Latin America is large, its populations are large, and there are a large lacunae in appreciation of what this sleeping giant could hold for both the New and the Old World. Perhaps that comprehension will be forthcoming before long, when the sleeping giant begins to stir.

Sincerely,

Shirley Hill Witt
(Akwesasne Mohawk)

* * * *

REFERENCES

(Note that most newspapers quoted are from Caracas, Venezuela).

1. "'No!' to Tourism and Colonization," *El Mundo,* 12/26/91.
2. "Trafficking in Indians," *El Nuevo Pais,* 01/15/92
3. "Dam Project Threatens Indian Tribe," by Nathaniel C. Nash, *New York Times News Service,* dateline Quepuca-Ralco, Chile, 02/14/92.
4. "People Cheating the Indians is Increasing," *El Globo,* 01/26/92.
5. "Ecuador's Indians Press Demands", *Washington Post,* 08/27/91.
6. "A Territory Reserved for the Yanomami Indians is Designated," *El Nacional* (EFE), 1/29/92; "A Dream Comes True for Venezuela's Yanomamis," story by Karen Krebsbach, *Daily Journal,* 09/24/91.
7. "First Strike by Indians", *El Nacional,* 09/26/91.
8. "Bari Indians Return Motors Donated by the Venezuelan Petroleum Bompany Maraven," *El Diario de Caracas,* 10/16/91.
9. "'Koreans are Taking Over Our Lands, say the Piaroa Indians'," *El Mundo,* 06/18/91.
10. "Tourists a Threat to Gran Sabana," *Daily Journal,* 06/30/91.

11.   "Indiscriminate Tourism is Promoted by the Governor of Amazonas Territory," story by Rita Ordonez, *El Mundo*, 07/16/91.

12.   "With Rituals to Frighten Away the Enemy, Yukpa and Bari Indians Prepare for Confrontations", *El Mundo*, 07/16/91.

13.   "Venezuela's Policy for Brazil's Gold Miners: Bullets," story by James Brooke, *New York Times*, 02/13/92.

14.   "The Cultivation of Poppies to Produce Heroin Invades Natural Areas," *El Universal*, 02/13/92.

15.   "Indian Communities Menaced by Urbanization", *El Universal*, 02/10/92.

16.   "Orinoco Delta Fauna are in Danger of Extinction", *El Globo*, 02/03/92.

17.   "Environmental Worries Kill Nicaraguan Logging Project," *Daily Journal* (UPI Story), 01/30/92.

18.   "Seems Sting Will Sing", *Daily Journal*, 01/29/92.

19.   "Kari'nas Demonstrate in Front of the Supreme Court of Venezuela Seeking to Reclaim Possession of Their Lands," *El Mundo*, 06/20/91.

20.   "Mapuche Indians Intend to Regain Their Lost Lands," *El Diario de Caracas*, 03/09/92.

21.   "Five Centuries of Ignominy", *Daily Journal*, 10/23/91.

22.   "Cocaine Barons Set Up Industry in Western Brazil," *Daily Journal*, 10/20/91.

23.   "Shotguns Exterminate Yanomamis," *El Nacional*, 10/19/91.

24.   "Dumped Mercury Poisons Amazon," *The Daily Journal*, 10/16/91.

25.   "Experts: Cholera May Devastate Amazon Tribes," AP Story, 05/03/91.

26.   "Argentina: President Menem Visited Cholera-Infested Province," *El Universal*, 02/10/92; "In Argentina, the Number of Cholera Victims Has Risen to 209", Bueno Aires (UPI Story), 03/03/92.

27.   "Explorer Shares Adventures", *Daily Journal*, Caracas, 03/01/92.

28.   "Emergency in the State of Zulia with 13 More Cholera Cases," *El Nacional,* 01/31/92.
29.   "Maracaibo Bus Terminal Held by Indians," *El Nuevo Pais,* 09/26/91.
30.   "In the Amazon, Diseases of Poverty Increase," El *Nacional,* 01/30/92.
31.   "Primitive Tribesman Lobbies for Money to Fight Disease," (AP story) The Daily Journal, 06/10/91.
32.   "More Than 40 Indians in the Delta Amacuro Territory Have Died From Malaria, Measles, and Tuberculosis," story by Rita Ordonez, *El Mundo,* 10/16/91.
33.   "Sao Paulo, Brazil: Indians of Brazil Have Killed Themselves to Protest Against Civilization", (AFP story *El Nacional,* 01/05/91.
34.   "Uncertain Future for Infants in the Delta Amacuro," *El Universal,* 08/30/91.
35.   "Using Shamans' Knowledge of Healing Plants," *Daily Journal,* 06/26/91.
36.   "Decree Reserves Venezuela Forest for Yanomamis", story by James Brooke, *New York Times News Service,* 09/17/91.
37.   "A Genetic Bank for Disappearing Indian Groups Proposed," *The Economist,* 09/07/91.
38.   "The Progress of an Aboriginal Community," datelined Amaicha Del Valle, Argentina, 02/14/91.
39.   "Reflections at the Turn of the Fifth Century Since the Meeting of Two Worlds," *El Universal,* 03/08/92.

Dear Christopher:

My name is Deborah Deaton (Athabaskan Indian/Alaska). I am a nineteen year old sophomore, attending the University of Alaska, Fairbanks. I was raised in Beaver, a small community of eight people. Your discovery of America didn't immediately affect the Athabaskan people where I'm from. However I feel close to all Native American Indians as if they are my fellow people. Therefore, I feel strongly about your "discovery."

You are undeniably an important man in history. In my eyes, it wasn't because you discovered the "New World" first. The Natives were living on it for thousands of years before you caught sight of it. I believe Natives should get more credit than they do now for the initial discovery of the "New World". What's ironic is the Vikings showed up five hundred years before you. Still history recognizes you as the man who discovered the "New World". Your voyage was important because Europe recognized it and continued contact with the "New World" afterwards.

Oh great "Admiral of the Sea" how contradictory is your mission! You want to save the world and get rich? You looked upon our land with greedy eyes pondering how you could profit from it. Your mission was launched "in the name of Jesus". Yet you treated us Native people with such cruelty. Was Native blood spilled in the name of God too? You, Columbus, are a hypocrite. You were going to bring Christianity to the naked people across the sea. But you were ultimately driven by your desire for gold...it was only mentioned in your journal 140 times.

What have you and your people done for the Natives? You have brought us small gifts like glass beads and hawk bells. From your visit you have left us diseases like small pox, whooping cough, and diptheria to remember you by. You have brutalized and enslaved the Natives while enriching yourself. I am angry that my fellow Native American Indians have been tortured, raped, and killed in the interest of progress. You have done so little for us, and hurt us so much more. Your discovery was of no benefit to us.

If anything I'm writing this letter to appeal to you conscience. I urge you to treat the Natives with respect. Treat them as you would want yourself to be treated in your new homeland.

It's important to remember not everyone lived "happily ever after" following your discovery. There were many Native people who died. I'm grieving over that loss. Writing this letter has helped me take another step towards healing.

Sincerely,

Deborah Deaton
(Athabascan)

Dear Christopher:

Reading through history I found your name
received significant credit for the discovery of the New
World in 1492. On the arrival to the New World, you placed
a Spanish Castile flag and called your discovery "San
Salvador or Holy Savior." The account mentioned that
neither you nor your crew suspected you discovered North
America. You thought that you reached the Indies rather
than the New World. With this assumption you called the
existing people of the land "Indians." This marked your
first encounters with the North American Indians.

The Indians paddled out to your ship and they
thought you were God. As you said "All believe that power
and goodness dwell in the sky...and they are firmly
convinced that I have come from the sky." By your own
judgement you considered the Indians were practicing
stone age customs.

Serving a Spanish monarch, your people had a
traditional requirement of newly discovered people that
read "If you do so...we shall receive you in all love and
charity." If this demand was rejected, the Spanish
promised: "We shall powerfully enter into your country,
and...shall take you, your wives, and your children, and
shall make slaves of them...the death and losses which
shall accrue from this are your fault." After your Spanish
crew read the proclamation, they shot in the air above the
Indians who were standing nearby. In response the
Indians took it as an attempt at war and a fight broke out.
Your Spanish people drove the Indians out of their land,
and held the broken survivors in contempt. A Spanish
priest described the scene as "Like the most cruel tygres,
wolves and lions, engrag'd with a shap and tedious
hunter." Between 1675-1876 with efforts at peace failing,
Indians and Europeans held the bloodiest war in

America's history where Europeans destroyed the Indian tribes. After the war, the population of Indians declined from approximately 60 million to 2 million.

As you well know the first human beings to set foot on the continent of North And South America were the ancestors of the modern Indians. The Indians were believed to come to North America tens of thousands of years ago during the Ice Age, a period in time during which a land bridge was believed to connect Northeast Asia with Alaska. The reason why Indians were believed to migrate was because they were gatherers and hunters, which led them to follow the animals who crossed over to Alaska.

If I understand the history books, the reason why the people who came after you flocked to America, was to find wealth and to get away from Christianity problems in England. In my opinion these reasons are not sufficient enough to kill off the innocent Indians even if they were considered as people still in the stone age. They could not have harmed you or anyone else without equipment, such as rifles.

I believe this era in history was not fair to the innocent Indians who were killed off, because the Indians respected the Europeans. In fact, they thought they were godlike people that were sent from the skies. The Europeans demoralized the Indians and destroyed their traditional values and customs. With this in mind I believe "Columbus" should not be a name to celebrate. Columbus! don't you think it is necessary to commemorate those poor innocent Indians who died in your battle and all the other battles rather than the remembrance of your hostility, cruelty, and greed? Besides the American Indians will never recognize a day in their lives when you were significant. They will remember their ancestors, who suffered and died in the battles. The invasions of their hunting grounds where

Dear Christopher

Europeans fought against each other to gain their own commonwealth.

If you could hear me, Columbus, I know your heart has no desires in celebrating yourself. If you're in good hands with our creator, you must be looking down on this earth and you must be visualizing the hate, anger and fighting which surrounds the world. It must look unpleasant. I personally think it is necessary to celebrate a world peace. The commemoration title should reflect a world awareness toward peace. Is that right, Columbus? In a dream you said "yes." In reality, you destroyed many dreams.

Sincerely,

Eunice P. Beans
(Alaskan Yupik)

Dear Christopher:

I'm Athabascan Indian from Stevens Village, Alaska. I am a Yukon River Rat (our nickname for Indians residing on the Yukon River). I was born back in the 1940's when rock was young and we were still a territory of the United States of America. My memories of becoming the 50th state are pretty vague. I just know, the Texans are still jacked-out of shape, considering they aren't living in the largest state anymore. I guess we cut them down to size; now they have nothing to brag about. While we were a territory, the land, rivers, lakes, and wild animals were shared equally by everyone. We were and still are abundantly supplied by the Great Spirit with moose, king salmon, bear, beaver, and muskrat. I would die for another taste of muskrat, unfortunately they are practically extinct. Christopher, The Loch Ness Monster would be a lot easier to find than a muskrat on the Yukon River drainage. Back then, people weren't on the sauce (alcohol or drugs) primarily because we had too much self-esteem and survival chores to attend to. Now it's sad to see our people depending on Uncle Sam (U.S. government) for handouts; welfare took our soul and medicaid took our limbs. I am truly grateful for my childhood memories in the village. The moonlit dogsled rides during the winter, fishcamp in the summer and winter picnics in the snow. The U.S. and all its rules, laws, and red tape can't take my memories from me.

I'll tell you what, Christopher, changing Alaska to a state was not my idea of being a happy camper. Alaska as a territory, sounds just fine to me. Forget about the heavy duty oil drilling, the annihilation of our people through big business, and by placing us on land the size of a postage stamp, plus giving us the hardships of becoming assimilated into a culture, which isn't even of our choosing.

Dear Christopher

Christopher, the history books portray you as such a hero who courageously braved the Atlantic Ocean, discovering America and giving us the name Indian. I also heard you were a gold digger. Is that true? Just trying to get the facts straight. You introduced greed, booze, disease, slavery, and your religious fanatics. The European Black Plague, couldn't have done a better job of wiping out the Native American Indians off the face of the continent. To this day, the assimilation of the American Indians hasn't been completed according to the Master Race plan.

Sorry to say, Christopher, your name is synonymous with the little guy in the red outfit, holding the pitchfork. I wonder, would you still be as enthusiastic to see if the earth was round, after reading this letter and hearing of the havoc you help to create on the North American continent.

Well, Chris Baby, maybe it's best you aren't around right now, because we still believe in lynching parties. I should say the deep south guys do. I'm not sure, but I think they're into lynching just about anybody. I have a lot more to discuss with you, maybe later.

Sincerely,

Donna John Sada-de-dwonethna
(Athabascan)

Dear Christopher:

The history books record that Christopher Columbus discovered America [on] October 12, 1492; those same history books also record that Vitus Bering discovered Alaska for Russia in 1741. How does the previous sentence make sense when isn't Alaska part of America? Since Mr. Columbus in fact rediscovered America and claimed it for Spain couldn't we say the same about Mr. Bering?

Would it be safe to say that Mr. Columbus discovered America or that he in fact discovered new people? Neither would be appropriate, and we can't even say that he discovered a distinct culture because there were so many separate aboriginal cultures scattered about North and South America at the time of his exploration. We could say that people have been discovering people for thousands of years before Columbus.

My people have lived on this continent for at least 11,000 years. However, I can't say that my forefathers discovered America, because due to archaeological findings along with carbon dating from ancient tools and implements found, there were Paleo Indian groups which includes the Algonquian and Aztecan language stocks here long before then. The Athabaskan and Eskimo languages were absent from the above-mentioned Native languages because they came later. How could Chris Columbus say he discovered this great continent when at the time of his landing he didn't even know where he was, and all he could prove at this time was that the earth was round. Maybe before his voyage he should have looked at the moon, and seeing that it is round, he would have to figure that the world would have to be round too.

The 500th anniversary celebration of Columbus' discovery of America next fall is an event that is frowned upon by Native Americans throughout the continental U.S. Martin Luther King Day is now beginning to be frowned upon by Native Alaskans. We as the first Alaskans feel that there should be a date celebrated that commemorates one of our own. Why can't we celebrate an event that was done by some Native Alaskan such as the first person ever to reach the summit of Mt. McKinley Walter Harper, who was an Athabaskan Indian and the first person ever to reach the summit of Mt. McKinley, was given credit for it locally, but we as Alaska Natives would question why he is not known nationwide. The original name for this great mountain which has the highest peak in North America is Denali which translates into "The Great One" in Koyukon Athabaskan. The mountain was perhaps given that name thousands of years before Columbus. However, the name is not used. Why? Because we can't have something that is Athabaskan named to be known nationwide? Yet we could allow our youngsters to see the name Columbus as someone who was an important figure in our history. I would say the name "The Great One" makes more sense than McKinley which was named after some past American president who didn't even see the mountain. At least Denali stands for something. Calling the mountain McKinley seems almost as absurd as naming Alaska's mountain sheep after William H. Dall an American explorer who in fact didn't even see these magnificent animals.

At Mt. Rushmore in South Dakota the monuments of four great presidents are in fact carved in stone that lies on the soil that has been taken by force and violence from the American Indians by white Americans who followed only a few hundred years behind Columbus. Since the first day of European occupation on American soil, there has been repeated devastation on the American Indians. If not directly then indirectly such as only a few famous Native Americans being recognized. Also the potato which originated from Native American Tribes is sometimes referred to as the Irish Potato. We as Americans give Columbus credit as a great explorer yet when Native Americans do something creative it is never recognized or its developers are questioned. The great Indian mounds that were discovered in the Mississippi Valley are spectacular works done by man, yet when the archaeologists first discovered them they determined that they could not have been done by Indians because they were made by people with far more creativity and intelligence.

A hundred and fifty years ago everyone including American Indians wanted to be known as white people. Today it is the direct opposite and many whites claim to be part Indian. There is the question of why one would say my great gramma was Indian rather than my great grandfather. Do they say that because they want their great grand parent to be an Indian princess rather than an Indian brave? We'll never know, be we as Indian peoples must hang onto our own dignity.

Whites such as Kit Carson or Daniel Boone have received about as much recognition as Columbus, and are read about in elementary school books as American frontiersmen and Indian fighters. What do statements like that do to the minds of Indian children? I'll tell you what it did to me; as a child I mistakenly viewed the noble red man as a savage race who deserved to be killed off. And because at the time the history books mainly focused on the white heroes, I traveled to the lower forty eight in 1968 with the impression that there were no Indians left, that they were all wiped out by our white American heroes. The history books have accounts of how the West was won in the name of freedom. There is hardly ever mention of the thousands of Indians who roamed the West freely before the coming of the whiteman.

Dear Christopher

Why is this country called the land of the free when many Indians are locked up on reservations? Most of the reservation lands selected were chosen by the Indians themselves and are in most cases suitable for growing crops. However, the Indian lands were reduced in size many times smaller than what the Indians were originally accustomed to. I think it would have been more appropriate to call this country the land that was once free for the American Indian. I would also like to mention that while many of the aboriginal people of the lower forty eight are known as American Indians or Native Americans, the Indians of Canada refer to themselves as first nation Americans. I think we should lobby to have that name placed on all Native Americans because it is the absolute truth.

American Indians after years of political protest are never really recognized as the discoverers of this country.   However, they are recognized in ways that ridicule them. The monument of Chief Crazy Horse of the Sioux on a horse that is being done in the Black Hills north of where the battle of the Little Bighorn, in which he took part, is only being done by a crazy whiteman who wants recognition for himself.   The Sioux who are descendents of this great chief do not want this monument done.

Why is Columbus who discovered American Indians so well known in history and why has he received so much attention while the people he discovered did not? The only recognition we get here in Alaska is that we are a race whose ancestors lived a simple lifestyle of hunting and gathering. If Columbus was here 500 years ago and tried to live like a native of that time I think he would have called it anything but simple.

Columbus may have been the first European white to make contact with the Native Americans but he is not the first white person to set foot on American soil. Eric the Red as he was known, had a son who explored what was believed to have been present day Newfoundland around 1000 A.D. There are also accounts of finding them later reconstructing what is believed to have been a 1000 year old Norse structure in Newfoundland. I wonder why these early day explorers didn't record their new discovered lands the way Columbus did? could it have been that they did not want to see a European invasion of this great land and its people? As a Native American that is what I hope they were thinking. Or could it be that Columbus was aware of it but chose not to reveal so that he could gain all the credit? That could hardly seem likely since Columbus set out on a venture to find a short cut to the Orient. Or did he?

In this day and age there are those who would argue that before the coming of the white man Alaska Natives suffered from starvation and extreme cold. In defence of these whitemen, these same people claim that our race was saved from hunger by the whites. My argument is that while many of our ancestors probably died of starvation, maybe it was meant to be that way so as to keep the race strong. I would argue that the white heroes of today who made starvation a thing of the past for Alaska Natives also introduced disasters similar to what Columbus introduced to those other Indians down south such as deadly diseases, alcoholism and poverty to our people to name but a few, of which we knew nothing about before.

Alaska was sold to America by Russians with no concern for the Natives and that it was their land that was really being sold. At the turn of the century when gold was being discovered in the remote areas of Alaska there was at the time no kind of land settlement made with the Alaska Natives. Even though it was on their soil that the gold was being extracted, no Natives were allowed to stake claims. Millions of dollars worth of gold was taken out of Alaska, which was not even a territory then, with no thought of giving the natives their share so that they could buy the whiteman's grub from the store shelves to keep their children from their so-called starvation. Did Columbus really discover America to create a great nation or was it really the start of destruction of the real American people whom he named Indians?

Again I would argue why famous Native Americans are not so well known by name as Columbus was. During World War II when the Japanese Intelligence kept breaking the secret codes used by the American forces, it was in fact descendents of the same Navajo Indians that Kit Carson tried to destroy who provided a solution. The U.S. armed forces used a secret code that was spoken in the Navajo language and the only reason why the Japanese couldn't break that code was because of the simple fact that they had no Navajo speakers. Now we all know that from the history books, but do we ever stop to think that if Kit Carson and other great Indian fighters as they were called had succeeded in wiping out the Indian, that the code would not have been made possible and while they may have found another solution, perhaps without the Navajo it would have taken them longer to win the war. As a Koyukon Athabaskan I am related to those very Navajo, but who's aware of that besides the historians, anthropologists and linguists.

Probably many of us have seen a picture of the statue of the five American Marines raising the flag after the taking of Iwo Jima in the West Pacific. How many know however, that one of those marines was in fact an American Indian Ira Hayes who was not only unharmed but also unnoticed? How many American citizens know that when our so called great American President at the time Harry S. Truman was praising the five marines that he completely ignored Hayes? You could probably imagine what this may have done to the Indians' dignity. One would wonder if Truman chose not to praise the American Indian hero whose ancestors were here long before Columbus, because he was sickened at what

American Indians have done to whites in the past. Or perhaps he was too ashamed of what whites have done to American Indians. One might also wonder why this American war hero who later died of alcoholism was so rejected by society after the war and he was not even welcome on the reservation.

During the late 1960s in Oklahome, you could still see notices on cafes or bar windows that stated "no Indians or dogs served here". That is not the case today but you still get discriminated against in different ways. I have an example of what happened to me in Fairbanks in 1975 during the height of the pipeline era. My late brother, myself, and a friend sat down in the Passtime cafe to eat and the waitress, who was a white woman, but I wouldn't call her a lady, refused to take our orders until we presented her with proof individually that we had the money. A little later a white male came in to eat, and we all noticed that she didn't ask him the same question. What kind of bigotry would Mr. Columbus call that in a country that he was supposed to have discovered?

I'm an honest person yet a white security guard once accused me of purse snatching at a hospital where I was once treated and have often made frequent visits to thank the nurses who helped in my recovery. I often wonder if it was because I am an Alaska Native that I was accused. People who have never been looked down upon the way I have often question me why I have so much hurt and anger inside me. These same people often preach to me that as a good Christian I have to learn how to forgive and forget. I try but sometimes I wish some whites would help me out by agreeing with me that we are of separate cultures who have different beliefs and values. Maybe we display our own methods of forgiving and forgetting. Maybe instead of trying to destroy Native religion early Columbus followers should have tried to educate their people to try to understand our beliefs the way they understood their own.

Dear Christopher

If Mr. Columbus were alive today, there are several things I would ask him, and one would be that as a Native American and proud of it, I would question by the Spanish had to study early American Indians to determine whether or not they were human. What did these first Americans look like if they didn't look human, could anybody tell me? I wonder if Mr. Columbus who lived 500 hundred years ago and who in fact brought some Native Americans back to Spain with him so that they may be baptized so that they would die Christians and go to heaven, was also aware of the fact that while all men were created equal to the eyes of God, that is not true among men. If Mr. Columbus were here today would he look back and say the same the same thing that the crew who dropped the atom bomb on Hiroshima said "oh my God what have we done!" If he were a Christian human like he claimed I think that is exactly what he would say, not because of what he's done but what he was responsible for starting.

Sincerely,

Phillip Albert Jr.
(Koyukon Athabaskan)

Dear Christopher:

DISCOVERY ERA

My spirit speaks to you from the past
when we first met
on the Caribbean Ocean shores.
You welcomed our sun and our warmth
upon your weary sea duck feet
and your weary tortured European souls
seeking freedom from its religious and hungry chains.
Haunted by many fearful, innocent pawns escaping
from the Royal Empire and the Pope's grasp.

You ached for comfort and freedom
yet memory ingrained from your good christian faith
saw only hell's chains in mine.
I saw your living spirit as free as mine that day.
You saw me as in darkness
and became blinded by my tan...
by my simple and uncomplicated ways.
You though you needed to free me.

The lands, the sea, the air
belonged to themselves.
The palms fell coconut abundantly,
the fish overflowed their cloudlike pattern
and you basked in the warm beaches
breathing in the turquoise ocean breeze.

At last feeling and being free.
Your need to claim, to control what was not yours
to obey your queen soon consumed you.
Consumed the land.

Ah, we must speak, we two.
We must set our forebears free

and those who come after us.
We must think of our future's future generation.
        Aaah, aaahhh, I am stabbed in the heart
                my huts on fire
                    my children slaves
                        great sickness came
                            their dying
                                50 million of

them.
In the first century.

                            Set us free.

        *   *   *   *

ONWARD WESTWARD ERA

My spirit from the "Human Beings"
who live from the east to the west speak to you.
Your great, great grandsons
four generations removed
have come into our plains, prairies, rivers and mountains
attacking.

What is this?...this way of yours
to doggedly grab and swipe and steal
to claim a tree, a river, a piece of land?
Why do you seek freedom?...and then not give back
as you first embraced on those ancient
Caribbean shores?

Their eyes only look within their own skin
as being the only right skin
and so many other yellow, red and black people
are burned, tortured and treated like dirt
so undeserving of a "human being"...
desecrating their living spirits.

Many treaties broken much like your own
swarming like moths of belongings.
The "white empire" eats and takes away
destroying my Creator's land
       not my land. Not yours.
Uncountable tribes, races of multicolored traces
forever gone with their treasured knowledge.
Trees cut forever causing vast deserts
never will be seen again.

Flaming homes charred by yours and my children's hands
four times removed
Tornadoes of change swept the vast lands
reshaping to what so many now-a-days call
the United States of America.
Freedom for some
       not worthy for others.

        *   *   *   *

MODERN ERA

My angry and resistant spirit
looks with cynical eye
at every selfish step toward progress,
economic growth and freedom
proposed.

The freedom that you sought
are screams, weeping and prayers of others now.
While your people boast of their free land and riches,
we cry of the violation
to dumb ears.

Strength of spirit and endurance of hardships
develop and mold their perpetual character

without their knowing,
Our great unseen Creator's hand
caught developing the true American spirit
of all freedom seekers
who want equal footing.

Question now is, at whose expense
will freedom and wealth reign?

My spirit is encouraged
by the changing and blending
of a multicolored traces of people
who fought and continue to fight
for what is truly just and right
of a free spirit in all.

The healing of the nation,
a people
a many rainbow colored people,
seeking to renew the damaged
soils, souls, and ancestral spirits.

Coming into a full circle
the voices of change
must quietly and harmiously acknowledge
with each other's ears and hearts,
in union only
can the Creator honor our attempts
to renew our, old twisted roots,
to renew our wilting earth
and to give birth to a "promised" future
for all our children.

    Sincerely,

    Nastasia K. Wahlberg
    (Yupik)

Dear Christopher:

I would like to take this time to share my thoughts with you and the emphasis on your recent sojourn with your discovery "Of A New World", and your statement that it is a new world inhabited by uncivilized savages.

I would like also for you to clarify what the statement of yours meant by your "Conquest". We have, or had not, or will not Cede, Give, Sell, Deed, Barter, Trade, or lease what is our God-Given aboriginal claim and right to the waters, forests, and lands of this spacious real-estate.

From the rising of the Sun in the East, to the setting of the Sun in the west, We in our latest census are 8-10-million people strong.

I would also like to point out that we have a strong complex family-oriented society. I can say that it's a concept that is "From The Womb To The Tomb." We take care of our own,--We are a maternal-paternal society.

We also are a law-abiding tribal affiliated honoring and clannish society and people. We respect the rights of our Brothers and Sisters to the North, East, South, and West. To live off the [land] and to partake of its lakes, streams, and rivers. This is a time-honored pledge of all the tribes across this great --country. Example, (The millions of Bisons roaming this country and the various fishes of its pristine waters)

We also have an agricultural program, (bar-none) that we grow what is indigenous to a certain area, which we have cultivated into a system of an annual harvest of our herbs, vegetables and staples which we utilize during the months of cold weather. These various staples we use in such different ways such as nutrition, medicine, and materials to make our blankets and clothes.

Also, as not to be irrelevant in regards to your uncouth statement of us as savages and uncivilized at that: We have an inherent and strong concept of a Creator, whom we identify and relate to, in a way, whom we honor and pay homage to with our songs, chants, dances and celebrations and tribal gatherings, where each tribe and indigenous people have their respective annual celebrations.

With that I shall close: May the Great Spirit guide you, your men, and the Nina, Pinta, and the Santa Maria over your route over the "Great Waters." And our humble greetings to your Queen Isabella and to King Ferdinand and may you always be "first in the hearts of your countrymen."

Sincerely,

Stephen R. Englishoe
(Gwich-Chyaa Gwichin Athabascan)

P.S. If you are planning a return trip, Please feel free to let us know and we will make "reservations", to accommodate you.

Dear Christopher:

I know you had good intentions when you came upon a group of people inhabiting this continent of America, while you thought you were in India. These Native Americans, as they are now usually referred to, have been called "Indians" for many years because it is the name you gave them and although most people are aware of this case of mistaken identity and the fact that "Indian" refers to India and not America, the name has stood.

I have also been lost and understand how easily it happens. As a ten-year-old child I was lost in the San Bernardino mountains, and like you, I did not possess a map. I had journeyed a great distance before I came to the realization that I was off my scheduled course. Yet, the consequences of my ordeal were all personal and no one besides myself and my family suffered.

On the other hand, your error in judgement has had profound effects on all peoples, especially Native Americans. Even since you "discovered" Natives, they have been treated as chattel. And although most Americans celebrate your national holiday with a day off of work and with a traditional family dinner of turkey, for Natives, Columbus Day is a national day of mourning.

My grandfather was raised on a Blackfeet reservation, yet, my family has tried very hard to hide their Indian heritage. They have preferred, because they were raised in the Hispanic community of Irwindale, California, to be thought of as Hispanic. Although, Hispanics are not generally held in high ethnic value, it is usually thought better to be Mexican than Native American.

When I finally turned around and walked in the opposite direction and retraced my footsteps and path I found my way back to camp and discovered by lone mother crying by a stream. I really wish you would have also discovered your error and turned completely around, as I did, but because you did not, it is not a single madonna who mourns...but a whole nation.

Sincerely,

Julie LaMay Abner
(Blackfeet/Cherokee)

Dear Christopher:

You ask us, the indigenous people of this nation, to take part in the celebration of your arrival and your "discovery" of America. I ask, "why?" There is irony in your request. Hypocrisy lies beneath the surface of your invitation.

The lives of my people is the breath that dried the ink on the government documents that stole this land away, piece by bloody piece. The ink on those documents is the blood of my people. What reason do we, as a conquered people, have to celebrate this day? What did you, Christopher, and your followers, do for my people? What contributions did your descendants make to my people's history, our culture, our way of life?

Our sacred land has been raped and torn apart. In its place, concrete monuments and asphalt freeways have been built. The bones of our people lie buried under trailer courts, swimming pools, high rise apartments and parking lots. The bones of our people have not been honored or respected. Instead, they have been dug up, trampled underfoot and kicked aside while looters and villagers searched for beads, baskets, and pottery. The bones of our people have been displayed in museums and carnival sideshows. The bodies of our leaders, elders, grandmothers and grandfathers have become glass-enclosed exhibits within the walls of universities.

Again I ask, why should Native Americans be asked to celebrate this day? Should I tell you of how my own people, the Cherokee, were forced to march from their forested homeland east of the Mississippi to the Darkening Land in the West, Oklahoma? Over 4,000 Cherokees died as a result of that particular death march, known as The Trail of Tears.

Dear Christopher

The destruction of my people, the Cherokee, is not unique in the history of Indian-white relations. The Pomo of California can tell you about the Bloody Island Massacre of their people around the area of Clear Lake (now a tourist resort and retirement area). Descendents of the so-called "Mission" Indians of Southern California can inform you about the enslavement and murder of their people under the Spanish mission system and the Franciscan priest, Father Junipero Serra. The Miwok and Maidu people can tell you about the mistreatment and murder of their people at the hands or under the instructions of Sacramento's "founder" Captain John Sutter. The Sioux people of the Dakotas can recount for you the massacre of their people at Wounded Knee. The Navajos can speak to you about their forced removal, remembered as The Long Walk, from their homeland in Arizona to the Bosque Redondo in New Mexico, at the hands of another Christopher --Christopher "Kit" Carson- -and the killing and starvation that accompanied them on their journey.

The history of Native Americans, since your arrival, is tragic--no cause for celebration. Should I rejoice for the death of my people across this nation, across 500 years, who were marched, murdered, hunted, shot down, strung up, put here, moved there, shifted about and turned inside out? Should I dance on the graves of my grandmothers, whose children were taken from their arms, placed in boarding schools, adopted out and crippled in spirit because they were not allowed to speak their language, sing their songs or remember their ancestors in the proper way? Should I bend my head in prayer, fold my hands, genuflect at the altar and give thanks to the "one nation under God" that tried to rob my people of their own gods--The Great Spirit, Grandfather, The Creator, Mother Earth?

Dear Christopher

What could "heathen savages" know about the concept of "do unto others?" What could "black devils" know about turning the other cheek, forgiveness, kindness, charity? We were told we had much to learn as we were made to sit in neat little rows, in neat little churches and adobe missions and "taught" the lessons of Christianity while they fed us from pig troughs, shaved the hair from our heads, beat our languages from our tongues, and replaced our tribal clothing with high, starched collars and tight laces. But we are a strong people, Christopher. We are still here. We have survived. We have survived the slaughter of our children and grandparents. We have survived the rape of our women. We have survived the theft of our land. We have survived removal. We have survived relocation. We have survived extermination. So, as you celebrate your arrival to these shores, we, the native people of this land will celebrate our survival as a people. We, as native people, will celebrate the visions and the silenced voices of our ancestors, whose eloquence went beyond words. We, as native people, will celebrate the wisdom and knowledge of our ancestors who spoke of what was to come, of what lay ahead, and who knew and believed in the concept of the never-ending circle--that what goes around, comes around. Yes, there is cause for celebration and commemoration, but not for the ideals expressed by your arrival or those later expressed by the concept of Manifest Destiny. We, the native people, will celebrate the voices we still hear and the visions we still see. We, the native people, will celebrate the fact that, despite everything, our heads are not bowed. Our backs are not broken. We are a strong and beautiful people--a Phoenix rising from the ashes.

Sincerely,

Yolanda Movita Tauzer
(Cherokee)

Dear Christopher:

message to columbus

the irony is that
400 years later the descendants of the
once *most beloved of god*
their blood mingled forever with the
progeny of Moctezuma
are the subjects of the errant descendants of their
most feared and dread enemies
and no better loved now than then
ah the fortunes of war and history
and even the offspring of your own forsaken
mother-land have fared little better
in this *new* world

the ghosts of the native children
cry piteously in their long night and
will now be exorcised by noisemakers and priests
already banished in history books and
extinct in the minds of most
yet

as a scholar
I'm not mad
because Europe was ripe for our *discovery*
and to tell you the truth
we fared little better under your
English brothers
the beggars of London
and their descendents
the Georgia crackers
who moved a once proud nation
into starvation and swamps
dispossessed and then drowned during removal
or under the ever popular "common man" president

who used us successfully in his military campaign
in the Louisiana swamps against the French
who did us the least harm
to launch himself into the presidency
before he denounced our race as a threat
to "decent" folk
never mind that some of us were already more literate
than he
or that historically we have all become
war bonnet-
war paint-wearing
savages
or listed as extinct in history books
or herded into concentration camps called reservation
and controlled by "degree of blood" like
so many ill-bred cattle

no
I'm not mad that you were a product of your culture
with all its own short-sightedness
after all
Moctezuma long toyed with the idea
that Cortez was really Quetzecoatl
and thus lost the "New World"
to a few unwashed Spaniards
and the rest of us long dallied before we resisted
hoping that perhaps...
well, none of them ever did go
home
how could we know that thousands upon thousands
of Europeans were starving
already living without dignity and hope
and that their only claim to superiority
would become their white skin
how could we predict
this alien culture
which valued land as a stepping stone to prosperity
land we had
but not in that sense

Dear Christopher

from its roots we sprang
and to its bosom we returned

to be fair
some who came did understand
mostly those who sprang from the earth themselves
and shared our sense of clan
they became one with us
so that our mingled blood stands proudly today
the product of many proud nations

I tell my son that he has five clans
his Navajo clan from his father
his Choctaw clan from his mother
and his Irish and Scottish clans from
all those bold explorers
who *joined with us*
long ago

the truth is that our histories are too mixed up
to sort out now
but your people could have been kinder to mine
sometimes at night I still cry for the children
frozen in those Arkansas swamps
who
in their right mind
would have sent naked children
in the dead of winter
into freezing swamps to die
that awful death
and what reasonable government would have called out
tanks to squelch a demonstration in South Dakota
or kept an innocent man jailed these long years for a
crime he didn't commit

for those of us who have suffered
this glorificaton represents a celebration of our
demise by an indifferent government
who has acted more the vulture than the eagle

Dear Christopher

in matters of race
but
what we may lack in number
we recover in spirit so that
like the legendary phoenix we rise
once again
guided by the ancestors
watching and planning
knowing all
they send us forth with the strength of survival
for after 500 years of continuous suppression
we are
still
and evermore

may your spirit rest
in peace
cristobo colombo
for the wheel of life
keeps turning
and we are here
still
and evermore

Sincerely,

George Ann Gregory
(Choctaw/Cherokee)

Dear Christopher:

Please regard this letter as a late notice for the bill you have left unpaid for 1250 generations. You have been remiss, disregarding every notice sent you. You have not paid us for the gold and silver your emissaries and commissioners removed from our coffers and resource base--bullion that rescued Europe from the Middle Ages, taking Europe into the modern world. Nor have you rendered compensation for the lands you appropriated and presently operate under new management without using or consulting any of the original proprietors in managerial decisions.

Mismanagement by your company's representatives has led to the depletion of the rain forest (actually, forests everywhere), exhaustion of farmlands, contamination from unwise resource extraction plans and extensive air and water pollution problems, not to mention punching a hole in the ozone layer as well as serious global warming trends that now threaten the planet. Your actions have exhausted our fishing industries, depleted our game reserves and ruined our indigenous markets.

Our legal department also informs us there is a case pending before the world's court for negligence on your part as well as your associate corporate raiders due to your transport of infective microbes leading to the wholesale accidental death of several million people. Reports of heavy raiding using the questionable practice of swords, long-bows and war dogs also concerns us, something we understand is now answerable before the United Nations.

Rumors and tabloids have also been linking the names of your representatives with illicit drug cartels and prostitution rings.   A number of your prominent managers are up on rape and slavery charges.   One unsavory account connects the names of your controllers and governors to unusual gaming practices involving human sacrifice of our citizens.

Labor practices have also come under scrutiny. Your New World employee work plans have not provided adequate health coverage, fair wage compensation, child labor compliance or worker safety. Indeed, work for your corporation has proven to be a death sentence. You have repeatedly appeared on OSHA's top ten list for violations. In addition, you have extended unfair advantage to your Catholic unionizers.   Equal opportunity must also be afforded to local union representation.

We also want to draw attention to indictments against your company for numerous patent violations. Our geneticists have been robbed of payment for their agronomic engineering of many commercially profitable varieties: maize, potatoes, beans, squash, tomatoes, yams, peppers and tobacco, to name only a few. Other products such as rubber, hemp, cotton, rice, and sorghums have also   proven   profitable   to   your   institutions--bitter harvests   for   us.   If   we   add   the   contributions   of pharmaceuticals and health practices developed by our indigenous practitioners to alleviate world suffering, surely we should have received Nobel Prize awards in every year since your arrival.

On a personal note, we've heard that you're suffering ill health at this time.   Please accept our condolences and might we make a suggestion. In light of your failing health, these criminal charges and legal actions, perhaps you should abstain from lavish celebration festivities planned for you this year.   You could better address your energies towards remedies within your company's internal structure that have

Dear Christopher

brought your corporation into a receivership position and pending bankruptcy.

Sincerely,

Sandra Lynch
(Inuit/Anishnabeg)

CONTRIBUTORS

Julie LaMay Abner (Blackfeet/Cherokee) is a graduate student and instructor of English literature and composition at California State University, San Bernardino. She is also research and editorial assistant to Dr. Rodney Simard (see below).

Phillip Albert, Jr. (Koyukon Athabaskan) is a student at the University of Alaska, in Fairbanks, and anticipates graduate work in Northern Studies and ultimately teaching in the Alaskan Native Studies Program at the University.

Charles G. Ballard (Quapaw/Cherokee) is currently Acting Director of the Institute for Ethnic Studies and an Associate Professor in the Department of English at the University of Nebraska at Lincoln.

Eunice P. Beans (Yupik) is a student at the University of Alaska, Fairbanks, and a strong believer in the maintenance of Native American dignity and unity.

Kimberly M. Blaeser (Anishinabe) is as Assistant Professor of English at the University of Wisconsin, Milwaukee and a professional writer. Her latest book, *Gerald Vizenor--Through the Oral Tradition* is to be published by the University of Oklahoma Press.

Sharon Manybeads Bowers (Assiniboine/Haida/Chippewa) is currently a graduate student in the American Studies graduate program at the University of Iowa. She is also a storyteller and is working on a play.

Ed Burbee (Luiseño) is a tribal leader on the Pachanga Indian Reservation near Temecula, California.

Charles C. Case (Nacirema) is a retired professor of anthropology at the University of Oregon. He is currently living in Tulare, California.

Peter David (Athabascan/Inupaiq) is a student at the University of Alaska in Fairbanks where he is majoring in Human Service Technology with the goal of becoming a substance abuse counselor.

Deborah Deaton (Athabaskan) is a student at the University of Alaska, in Fairbanks.

Stephen R. Englishoe (Gwich-Chyaa Athabaskan) is a native of Alaska and has lived all his life on the banks of the Yukon River. He has been involved with his local Native Village Council and various agricultural projects.

Marcelle Gareau (Metis) is a student in the Department of Anthropology at the University of Alberta, in Edmonton, Alberta (Canada).

Karl E. Gilmont (Coharie) is a teacher, writer, Native American studies consultant, and pow wow dance judge in Anthony, New Mexico.

Dave Gonzales (Yaqui) is a novelist and professor of English at Bemidji State University at Bemidji, Minnesota. He also teaches American Indian Philosophies for the American Indian Studies Department at the University of Minnesota in Minneapolis.

Janice Gordon (Blackfeet) and **Karen Neumiller** (Assiniboine) are students at the University of Montana in Missoula.

George Ann Gregory (Choctaw/Cherokee) is completing her Ph.D. at the University of New Mexico. Her goal is to

become both a poet and a scholar while working for better
education for minorities.

Michael James Hormann (Inupiaq) has lived "in and
around" Fairbanks, Alaska, for most of his life. He holds
a B.A. in psychology and his favorite pasttime is
"nighttime sky-gazing."

M. Annette Jaimes (Juaneño/Yaqui) is a lecturer in
American Indian Studies at CSERA, currently on leave at
the Society for the Humanities at Cornell University
where she is pursuing post-doctoral study on the structure
of scientific racism.

Rita Joe (Micmac) is a professional writer whose works
include *LNU and Indians We're Called, Songs of Eskasoni,
and Poems by Rita Joe.*

Donna John (Athabaskan) is a student at the University of
Alaska, Fairbanks, and intends to pursue an advanced
degree in Art Therapy.

Joseph W. Leonard (Miami) is in the School of Business
Administration at Miami University in Oxford, Ohio,
where he is in the Department of Management. His
specialities are strategic management, and international
and East Asian business.

Sandra Lynch (Inuit/Anishnabeg) is a graduate student in
anthropology at the University of California, Riverside.

Lewis W. Malatore (Yakima/Cree), **Joseph G. Hamelin**
(Blackfeet/Cree), and **Marilyn Skahan-Malatore**
(Yakima/Quinault) are students at the University of
Montana, in Missoula.

Glenn McGuire (Pawnee) was taken from his Pawnee
mother as a child by by white relatives and sent away to
Haskell Indian School in Lawrence Kansas. He now lives

in Riverside, CA., where he taught at Sherman Indian Institute for 14 years. His first book, a volume of poetry entitled *Spider Spins Between Two Worlds* was published by the American Native Press Archives of the University of Arkansas Press. McGuire says that his ambition has always been to write the Great Native American novel.

Yvonne Metivier (Oneida) is a resident of Pasadena, California and is involved in Native American activities both nationally and in Southern California.

Ronald Mossholder (Osage) has enjoyed a varied career in construction management on domestic and foreign projects, service in both WWII and in Vietnam, houseboat retirement, and, currently, is a construction business manager in Saudi Arabia while considering a second retirement.

Charles C. Muzny (Cherokee) is a lecturer for the Department of Anthropology and the American Indian Studies Program at California State University, Northridge.

Joseph W. Presley (Choctaw) is Dean of the College of Arts, Sciences, and Letters at the University of Michigan at Dearborn.

Paul Rice (Creek) is poet, author of stories and essays, and Associate Professor of English at the University of S outh Carolina/Coastal Carolina College. He is also an accomplished flint knapper.

Shawnele Root (Wasco/Tlingit) is a student at the University of Montana in Missoula.

Mary Gordon Sellers and **David Gordon** (Blackfeet) are students at the University of Montana in Missoula.

Rodney Simard (Cherokee) is a member of the Department of English at California State University, San Bernardino, where he among other courses, he teaches American Indian literature and Shakespeare.

Georges E. Sioui (Huron/Wyandot) is currently a member of the faculty at the Saskatchewan Federated Indian College at the University of Regina in Regina, Canada.

Yolanda Movita Tauzer (Cherokee) is raising a family and pursuing a graduate degree in history at California State University in Sacramento. Her professional goal is to teach Native American history at the college level and "to tell the truth."

John Torres (Navajo) is currently a graduate student in anthropology at the University of California, Riverside. His mother and maternal grandmother were both a part of a Native People assimilation program.

Nastasia K. Wahlberg (Yupik) is a student at the University of Alaska, Fairbanks, and hopes to become a professor writer and educator.

Samantha Whitefeather (Chippewa) is twelve years old and lives in Milwaukee, Wisconsin.

Darryl Babe Wilson (Pit River) is a graduate student in literature at the University of Arizona and a professional writer. His works have been included in *Talking Leaves*, *Earth Song_*, and *News from California.*

Shirley Hill Witt (Akwesasne Mohawk), an anthropologist, was working as a Foreign Service Officer serving with the United States Information Service in Caracas, Venezuela. She is now retired and living in Albuquerque.